# Early Developmental Hazards: Predictors and Precautions

# AAAS Selected Symposia Series

Published by Westview Press
5500 Central Avenue, Boulder, Colorado

for the

American Association for the Advancement of Science
1776 Massachusetts Ave., N.W., Washington, D.C.

# Early Developmental Hazards: Predictors and Precautions

Edited by
Frances Degen Horowitz

*AAAS Selected Symposia Series*

Published in 1978 in the United States of America by

   Westview Press, Inc.
   5500 Central Avenue
   Boulder, Colorado 80301
   Frederick A. Praeger, Publisher and Editorial Director


Library of Congress Number: 78-352
ISBN: 0-89158-084-0


Printed and bound in the United States of America

# About the Book

*This volume examines the importance of prenatal, birth, and postnatal factors in determining the extent of "risk" that may be predicted for an infant in the first year of life and in early childhood. It offers the reader an up-to-date review of major research efforts toward understanding the circumstances that insure optimal developmental opportunities for all children. In the first chapter, Dr. Horowitz presents some of the basic issues concerning vulnerability of young infants and developmental hazards. Papers by Arnold Sameroff and Herbert Leiderman consider early infant-environment interactions as they relate to normal developmental processes and social bonding. Lewis Lipsitt examines data from the Collaborative Perinatal Project and from studies on Sudden Infant Death Syndrome to propose some factors that contribute to the SIDS phenomenon. Trygg Engen reviews his research on the conditions that influence children to ingest harmful substances. The concluding chapter considers the implications of these papers for understanding environmental and biological conditions as they affect the developmental course of the infant and young child.*

# Contents

# List of Tables

# Foreword

The *AAAS Selected Symposia Series* was begun in 1977 to
provide a means for more permanently recording and more
widely disseminating some of the valuable material which is
discussed at the AAAS Annual National Meetings.  The volumes
in this *Series* are based on symposia held at the Meetings
which address topics of current and continuing significance,
both within and among the sciences, and in the areas in which
science and technology impact on public policy.  The *Series*
format is designed to provide for rapid dissemination of information, so the papers are not typeset but are reproduced
directly from the camera copy submitted by the authors, without copy editing.  The papers are reviewed and edited by
the symposia organizers who then become the editors of the
various volumes.  Most papers published in this *Series* are
original contributions which have not been previously published, although in some cases additional papers from other
sources have been added by an editor to provide a more com-
prehensive view of a particular topic.  Symposia may be reports of new research or reviews of established work, particularly work of an interdisciplinary nature, since the AAAS
Annual Meeting typically embraces the full range of the
sciences and their societal implications.

WILLIAM D. CAREY
*Executive Officer*
*American Association for*
*the Advancement of Science*

# Preface

This volume of papers is based upon a Symposium presented at the meetings of the American Association for the Advancement of Science in Denver, Colorado during February, 1977. The Symposium was sponsored by the Society for Research in Child Development in conjunction with Section J (Psychology) of the AAAS.

Preparation of this volume was made possible by the cooperation of the staff of the College Support Services Center of the College of Liberal Arts and Sciences at the University of Kansas. The contributions of Pamela Dane and Nancy Kreighbaum in setting and typing the manuscript are gratefully acknowledged. Vicki Czernicki's work in preparing the indexes was invaluable.

The topic for the Symposium was originally suggested by Lewis P. Lipsitt who has long served as the "arranger" for the AAAS Symposia that have occurred under the sponsorship of the Society for Research in Child Development. His cooperation and the cooperation of the other symposium participants has been appreciated. It is hoped that this volume will find interested readers who share with us the excitement of a currently vigorous research area.

Frances Degen Horowitz
August, 1977

# About the Editor and Authors

*Frances Degen Horowitz is a professor in the Departments of Human Development and Psychology and associate dean of the College of Liberal Arts and Sciences at the University of Kansas. She is also a research associate with the Bureau of Child Research at the University and president of the Division of Developmental Psychology of the American Psychological Association (1977-1978). Her areas of specialization are infant behavior and development, early intervention, and children's learning; she is the author of some 50 papers in these fields and the editor of* Monographs of the Society for Research in Child Development.

*Trygg Engen is professor of psychology at Brown University. His main interests are psychophysics and olfaction, and he is the author of over 50 publications in these areas.*

*P. H. Leiderman, professor in the Department of Psychiatry and Behavioral Sciences, specializes in psychiatry and child development. He is the coauthor of* Culture and Infancy: A Comparative Psychological Perspective *(Academic Press, 1977) and has written articles on mother-infant relations.*

*Lewis P. Lipsett is professor of psychology and medical science and director of the Child Study Center at Brown University. He has conducted research on infant development, learning processes of infants, and perinatal factors and developmental deficits, and is currently investigating crib-death infants and the perinatal correlates. He is the editor of* Developmental Psychobiology: The Significance of Infancy *(Lawrence Erlbaum Associates, 1976).*

*Arnold J. Sameroff, professor of psychology, pediactrics and psychiatry at the University of Rochester, has studied learning in infancy and the developmental consequences of perinatal factors.  He is the author of numerous articles on these topics and is currently writing a monograph on early development.*

# Early Developmental Hazards: Predictors and Precautions

# The Human Infant and the Processes of Development

Frances Degen Horowitz

The set of papers in this volume was originally presented as part of a symposium at the 1977 meetings of the American Association for the Advancement of Science. While each paper speaks to its own topic it may be helpful to set the papers against a broader context of the history of the problems that have been taken up by scientists interested in understanding early human development.

When the scientific study of human development began in earnest in the late 1800s one of the natural sources of information was to be found in observations of the development of the human infant. In the early diaries of the "baby-watchers" was recorded some of the basic information about regularities of development and dynamic forces of change (Wright, 1960). When the first questions about the process of learning and perception were being asked scientists found some answers in early experiments with human infants. Valentine (1914) used honey as a reinforcer to study color perceptions and preferences in young infants. When the nature-nurture controversy enjoyed its initial formulations in this century experimental, naturalistic, and correlational studies involving human infants were conducted in the hope that with the inexperienced, seemingly biologically pristine organism answers would be found. In Watson and Raynor's work on conditioning (1920) and in Gesell's work on maturation vs. learning (Gesell, 1954) the human infant served as subject. Many investigators turned to the human infant in the hope that simple questions could be asked so as to illuminate the relative contributions of heredity and of environment. (See Osofsky, In press and Stone, Smith, and Murphy, 1973 for basic reviews of research).

Despite the extensive amount of early research on the behavior of the human infant most developmental scientists thought of the the infant as a relatively primitive organism, governed by reflexive behavior and indiscriminatively responsive. Though there was much to be learned that would contradict this, it was as if the scientists studying the human infant were blinded by their own intentions. For, it is probably the case that many of the investigations involving human infants in the first four decades of this century chose the infant for the convenience of the question rather than for intrinsic interests in infant behavior: Nature vs. nurture, maturation vs. learning, parameters of conditioning. The major exceptions were the descriptive studies which charted the course of development. A further exception was to be found in the work of the Swiss psychologist, Jean Piaget and in the theoretical propositions of Sigmund Freud. But Piaget's work was to have an impact several decades later and Freud's analyses did not produce a large body of empirical work with infants.

Just before the beginning of the Second World War some of the most animated controversies on the nature-nurture question were shelved. This occurred partly because it became clear that the methodological techniques available at the time were inadequate to the questions. Some of the most extensive studies on conditioning were terribly vulnerable to methodological critique; similarly, the experimental manipulations aimed at affecting developmental outcome were subject to severe criticism. With the onset of the war most of the scientific energies of the world were turned away from the study of behavior. It was not until after the war with the training of a new generation of developmentalists that many of the issues would be addressed again. In the late 1950s and in the early 1960s, now armed with the technological advances that permitted automatic data recording and sophisticated observational techniques, better equipped with statistical and other data analysis paradigms, and supported by the thinking and research on animal behavior, developmentalists were able to turn back to the human infant and enter into an era of incredible productivity. Fueled by both theoretical formulations and empirical investigations and stimulated by natural interdisciplinary consortiums we have benefitted from more than 20 years of extraordinary advances. The result is that our entire perspective about the human infant has changed drastically. We have come to understand that the infant is competent and complex (Stone, Smith, and Murphy, 1973; Appleton, Clifton, and Goldberg, 1975); we have come to understand, as well, that our questions concerning development must mirror the complexity of the phenomena we are studying (Horowitz, 1977); and we have, ironically, been able to rephrase the original questions for which the human infant was a convenient subject to more sophisticated questions which <u>require</u> that the human infant be the necessary focus.

For the reader who is not familiar with the manner in which we can now characterize the human infant a brief overview might prove helpful. The human newborn can see and discriminate among visual stimuli (Fantz, 1963); the normal newborn responds to many auditory stimuli (Graham, Clifton, and Hatton, 1968); the human newborn can be conditioned (Lipsitt, 1963; Siqueland and Lipsitt, 1966); and the human newborn is sensitive to olfactory and tactile stimulation (Self, Horowitz, Paden, 1972; Engen and Lipsitt, 1965). It is possible to test the newborn infant generally (Brazelton, 1973; Self and Horowitz, In press; Rosenblith, In press) and it is possible to study sensory and learning processes in the first few days of life (Lipsitt, 1977).

Going back further in the developmental process we have also come to appreciate that the nine months of gestation is not a protected period during which the developing organism is isolated from environmental influence. Drug ingestion, infection, smoking, alcohol intake and nutritional unsufficiency have been shown to influence the pre-natal course and to predispose the infant to developmental risk (Lubchenko, 1976). The birth process itself, long known to be a hazardous set of events has provided clues to developmental prognosis. The modern usage of obstetrical medication seems to compound matters (Brackbill, In press; Horowitz, et al. 1977).

While environmental impact during the gestational period looks increasingly significant, biological pre-dispositions and genetic factors are not discounted for their influences (Freedman, 1974). Exactly how the environmental and biological factors interact during the prenatal period is not well understood. That we must be as concerned with the interaction prenatally if we are to understand the human newborn as we have been concerned about the interaction of these factors postnatally for understanding development during infancy and beyond is now much more fully appreciated than it was even a decade ago.

At birth, then, we have a complex organism that has journeyed through a nine month history. We also have a competent organism capable of processing information and affecting its environment. Yet birth is obviously a beginning and the development that lies ahead is a challenge both for the organism and for the scientist attempting to understand. There is the challenge to predict and, ultimately, to intervene and affect the course of development. Our society concurs in the ideal of safeguarding the developmental opportunities for every child born into our midst. The questions that we formulate must at one and the same time test the simple propositions and address the complex issues. In the papers in this volume we have examples of just this dual requirement.

The first two papers focus upon some specific processes in relation to fatal and lethal dangers that beset the infant and the young child. Lewis Lipsitt takes the topic of the Sudden Infant Death Syndrome and examines data from thousands of infants looking at the interaction of precursors and failure to learn. His analysis moves us one step closer to shedding the aura of mystery from a phenomenon that takes the lives of 10,000 infants a year in the United States. Trygg Engen applies the techniques of the experimental study of olfaction and taste to the problem of preventing the ingestion of harmful substances by young children. His treatment provides the necessary cautions of assuming that the infant's ability to discriminate and even to reject substances necessarily prevents harmful ingestion when the child comes into natural concourse with the substances. The processes of learning and strategies to maximize opportunities to learn what will safeguard the child must, therefore, become part of our protective concerns for the developing child.

The third and fourth papers in this volume are concerned with the parameters and functions of the interactive or transactive processes in which the infant is involved from birth onward. P. H. Leiderman examines some of the things that happen in the neonatal period with regard to the social bonding of the newborn infant and its mother. He questions recent assertions that the neonatal period is a critical period for the establishment of social bonding for all mother-infant pairs and suggests that the social bonding phenomenon may have a more variable period for establishment. Developmental progress may depend as much upon the factors which maintain social bonding after its initial establishment as upon the first occurrences. Arnold Sameroff's paper goes beyond the newborn period by reporting results from the Rochester Developmental Psychopathology Study. He tries to trace complex interactional patterns from the newborn to preschool period and provides evidence for asserting that the largest impact upon the intellectual and social competence of the preschool child can be traced to environmental factors transmitted through mother-child interaction patterns.

Recent and current research with human infants is proceeding along a number of diverse lines. Some of these involve investigations limited to a few variables or intensive analyses of particular phenomena; others take in a larger set of variables and address more global questions. It would be a mistake to view the studies aimed at limited and intensive analyses as being less significant than those which appear to take on broader issues. Developmental outcome is complex at best; understanding the threads, themes, and interactions that weave the developmental fabric will require many different types of investigations covering the spectrum from narrow to wide focus. The papers in this volume, in some ways, represent a sample across this spectrum of investigative strategies. Yet, each of the papers can be thought of as converging, finally, upon the theme of developmental hazard. The clues they are identifying may permit us to develop effective means of prevention and intervention in safeguarding developmental opportunities for every child.

The developmental journey for the human organism begins with conception and ends with death. Few modern humans reach the Biblical 120 years; yet, if we cannot reasonably aspire to such a length of days  70 to 80 years  of productive life is increasingly an expectation. For some humans 70 years are truncated significantly  or so  affected as to result in non-productive lives.  Early experiences and early processes  are  probably  important determiners  of the nature of the days one lives out.  To the extent that our data enable us to predict,  and  take action  we  shall  be  enabled  to  provide the necessary safeguards that increase the probability that  the  newly conceived  fetus  will grow to a healthy, productive, and happy adulthood.  In the papers in this volume  you  have an  excellent  sample  of  some  of  the current research relating to these issues.

## References

Appleton, T., Clifton, R., and Goldberg, S. The development of behavioral competence in infancy. In F. D. Horowitz (Ed.) Review of Child Development Research. Vol. 4. Chicago, Ill.: University of Chicago Press, 1975, 101-186.

Brackbill, Y. Obstetrical medication and infant behavior. In J. D. Osofsky (Ed.) Handbook of Infant Development. N.Y.: Wiley, In Press.

Brazelton, T. B. Neonatal Behavioral Assessment Scale. London: William Heinemann Medical Books, 1973.

Engen, J. and Lipsitt, L. P. Decrement and recovery of responses to olfactory stimuli. Journal of Comparative Physiology and Psychology, 1965, 59, 312-316.

Fantz, R. Pattern vision in newborn infants. Science, 1963, 140, 246-297.

Freedman, D. Human Infancy: An Evolutionary Perspective. N.Y.: John Wiley, 1974.

Gesell, A. The ontogenesis of infant behavior. In L. Carmichael (Ed.) Manual of Child Psychology, N.Y.: Wiley, 1954.

Graham, F., Clifton, R. K., and Hatton, H. Habituation of heart rate responses to repeated auditory stimulation during the first five days of life. Child Development, 1968, 39, 35-52.

Horowitz, F. D. Stability and instability in the newborn infant: The quest for elusive threads. Paper delivered at 1977 meeting of the Society for Research in Child Development.

Horowitz, F. D., Ashton, J., Culp, R. E., Gaddis, E., Levin, S., and Reichmann, B. The effect of obstetrical medication on the behavior of Israeli newborns and some comparisons with American and Uruguayan infants. Child Development, 1977, 48, In Press.

Lipsitt, L. P. Learning in the first year of life. In C. C. Spiker and L. P. Lipsitt (Eds.) Advances in Child Development and Behavior. N. Y.: Academic Press, 1963.

Lipsitt, L. P. The study of sensory and learning processes of the newborn. Clinics in Perinatology Vol. 4. #1, March, 1977, 163-186.

Lubchenko, L. The High Risk Infant. Philadelphia, Pa.: 1976.

Osofsky, J. (Ed.) Handbook of infant development. N. Y.: Wiley, In Press.

Rosenblith, J. The Graham Rosenblith Behavioral Examination for Newborns: Prognostic value and procedural issues. In J. Osofsky (Ed.) Handbook of Infant Development. N.Y.: Wiley, In Press.

Self, P. A. and Horowitz, F. D. Neonatal assessment: An overview. In J. D. Osofsky (Ed.) Handbook of Infant Development. N. Y.: Wiley, In Press.

Self, P., Horowitz, F. D., and Paden, L. Y. Olfaction in newborn infants. Developmental Psychology, 1972, 1, 349-363.

Siqueland, E. and Lipsitt, L. P. Conditioned head-turning behavior in the newborn. Journal of Experimental Child Psychology, 1966, 3, 356-376.

Stone, J., Smith, H., and Murphy, L. (Eds.) The Competent Infant. N. Y.: Basic Books, 1973.

Valentine, C. W. The colour perception and colour preferences of an infant during its fourth and eighth months. British Journal Psychology, 1913-14, b, 363-386.

Watson, J. B. and Raynor, R. Conditioned emotional reactions. Journal of Experimental Psychology, 1920, 3, 1-14.

Wright, H. F.  Observational child study.  In P. H. Mussen (Ed.) Handbook of Research Methods in Child Development.  N. Y.: John Wiley and Sons, 1960, 71-139.

# Perinatal Indicators and Psychophysiological Precursors of Crib Death

Lewis P. Lipsitt

Crib death, or the sudden infant death syndrome, takes perhaps as many as 10,000 babies a year in the United States alone. It is the single most common "cause" of death in the first year of life, excluding the especially hazardous first few days after birth. The peak incidence is between the ages of two and four months of age, and there is seasonal variation, with peaks in the winter or spring for the United States. Ninety per cent of crib death cases occur before six months of age, and 99 per cent before one year. Almost every case of sudden infant death syndrome (SIDS) occurs during a sleep period, and the infants are usually found in the morning after no apparent sign of struggle. Babies who succumb to crib death simply stop breathing, at least as far as most later inquiries can determine. There is usually no evidence of any agonal experience, no sign of pain or struggle. Interestingly, and undoubtedly significantly, a mild upper respiratory infection is found in 40-50 per cent of the cases, with the parents reporting a runny nose, raspy breathing, and so on. There is seldom any fever. The baby has been regarded in the few days immediately preceding the death as essentially normal.

The fallout from crib death in grief, despair, and loneliness among the thousands of close survivors is a further tragedy, especially in the absence of definitive answers regarding the basic mechanisms underlying SIDS. Crib death may be properly regarded as a public health menace in terms of the numbers of persons grievously affected by it. The tragedy is compounded by the chronic lack (until recently) of research attention to the nature of the disorder, among medical scientists, sociologists, and psychologists, to all of whom it should be of great scientific and humane interest, and by the frequent

11

popular confusion of the sudden infant death syndrome with child abuse.

We need to know more about the precursors of crib death. The first line of defense against it would be to define those conditions that seem present, prior to the death, in those infants that have succumbed. Descriptions of such conditions, in the absence of satisfactory explanations, would be useful at this stage of our understanding (Protestos et al., 1973). Even the casual and necessarily anecdotal report of psychophysiological attributes of infants who have been "near misses" would, or might, provide a lead into the psychobiological processes that may be operating in infants that die.

Although there has been a shroud of mystery associated with the sudden infant death syndrome, which has tended to preclude the avid investigation of its causes, some investigators in recent years have been able to document psychophysiological conditions which are correlated with SIDS. While the mechanisms and processes underlying crib death are not by any means clear at this time, there are tempting signs on the scientific horizon to suggest that a better understanding of the phenomenon is not far off. Steinschneider (1976), for example, has been showing persistently that apnea, or the spontaneous interruption of respiration, is a significant factor in the origins of SIDS. He believes that those infants who are particularly prone to apneic conditions during sleep are those who subsequently succumb to crib death. Thoman et al., (1976) have also presented data suggesting that a respiratory anomaly is involved. The notion that respiratory peculiarities are involved in crib death has been around for a long time. Crib death was at one time thought due to overlaying, the condition in which the mother inadvertently rolled over on her infant during sleep, causing smothering. There are anecdotes, also, of instances in which an infant was offered a cloth, apparently soaked in something sweet, to suck on as a pacifier or perhaps to reduce teething discomfort; crib death was sometimes attributed to choking on the cloth. In more recent times, smothering has persisted as the popular interpretation of such deaths. This interpretation has exacerbated parental grief, for the suggestion of "suffocation" often carries with it the burden of presumed negligence on someone's part. It is seldom considered, or has been seldom considered until now, that smothering may occur as readily, if not more so, from endogenous causes as from external stimuli.

Recent evidence of Emery and his colleagues in England (Protestos et al., 1973), of Naeye, Ladis, and Drage (1976), and of Anderson and Rosenblith (1971) support the respiration aberration hypothesis. Those infants who subsequently die of sudden infant death syndrome, while ostensibly normal according to most visible criteria of infant well-being, have endured histories of obstetrical/perinatal/neonatal stresses which could dispose them to "unexplained death" two or three months hence, and which do implicate respiratory problems.

We have data from a retrospective study of crib deaths in Providence which further support the proposition that respiratory abnormalities were present at birth, months before the infants died. The data to be presented here (Lipsitt, Sturner, & Burke, 1977) like those of Naeye et al. (1976) contribute to a picture of crib death as a subtle debility which apparently sets the stage for the later development of a specific breathing deficit. The thesis which I will propose is that perinatal hazards and congenital debilities of the fetus and newborn may place the infant in special jeopardy, in that any early behavioral deficits will be compounded by the failure of experience to prepare the infant for later threats to its survival. Infants who as newborns are incapable of responding defensively to stimulus hazards will be especially vulnerable at later ages, e.g., at two to four months of age, by which time the infant must learn certain defensive postures and respiratory responses that will reduce the threats to survival from smothering or suffocation. The proposition presented here is that crib death might be a learning disability secondary to a congenital incapacity to properly divert threats to respiratory occlusion. First, the constitutional aspects of crib death:

In one recent study of the developmental histories of crib death (Naeye, Ladis & Drage, 1976), 125 SIDS victims were compared with matched controls. The data for this study were from the Collaborative Perinatal Project of the National Institute of Neurological and Communicative Disorders and Stroke in which eleven cities throughout the nation were represented. The targets of study were all born between 1959 and 1966. The investigators compared the 125 SIDS cases with over 50,000 infants of the Collaborative Study who were born alive and survived the early months of life. This "unmatched control group" was supplemented by another "matched control group" of 375 infants, matched with the victims for place of birth, date of delivery, gestational age, sex, race, and socio-economic status. All of the matched controls were "sur-vivors." Infants with major congenital anomalies were excluded both in the SIDS and the matched control categories.

The study found multiple signs of possible neonatal brain dysfunction in future SIDS victims. Abnormalities were documented in respiration, feeding, temperature regulation, and specific neurologic tests. Apgar scores were significantly lower in the future victims. There was a greater incidence of maternal influenza and cigar-ette smoking of mother in the histories of infants who succumbed, a finding made also by Bergman and Wiesner (1976). SIDS victims, moreover, had a greater proportion of young mothers of low socioeconomic and educational level, who lived in crowded housing, and had minimal pre-natal care. In the Naeye et al. study, a greater propor-tion of the SIDS victims were underweight at birth for gestational age. There was little or no suggestion in the histories of any hereditary influence predisposing to crib death. It was noted by Naeye et al. that many of the crib death victims who grew normally prenatally were growth-retarded following birth, probably not as a result of undernutrition.

The Naeye et al. study was a very large investigation based upon the computerized medical records of thousands of births occurring across the country. One may question whether such differences between SIDS and control cases would appear in smaller, "local" groups of potential SIDS victims and under conditions in which the SIDS victims are matched one-for-one with the next birth of the same sex and race occurring in the same hospital. Such a study was undertaken in Providence. The epidemiological or actuarial statistics relating paranatal character-istics to later crib death are borne out by a study

(Lipsitt, Sturner, & Burke, 1977) of the 15 crib death cases in the Providence sample of the National Collaborative Perinatal Project. Studying the 15 Providence cases (of 4,000 births) diagnosed by Naeye as true crib deaths, the Providence group confirmed that there were pathological precursors which could provide the basis for a predictive scale of developmental jeopardy in relation to SIDS, even during the newborn period. Neonatal psychophysiological factors, it was concluded, might well be involved in the final pathway to the condition that ultimately causes the death of the infant, usually between two and four months of age. By psychophysiological factors is meant not only simply autonomic nervous system deficiency, although that would be part of the story, but the effects which early experiences may have on the very young child and which experiences may affect the child's later ability to cope with stressful stimulation.

We began with the records of those 15 true SIDS cases identified by Naeye, and then selected a control group of cases which was comprised of the very next birth, of the same sex, into the project. The child was born in the same hospital, usually on the same day as the target or deceased case. We compared this control group with the SIDS group and immediately found that a second control group was required, for while there were seven infants in the deceased group that were non-Caucasian, there were two in the "matched" control group. A third cohort was therefore identified, this consisting of the subsequent births into the study of both the same sex and race. The apparent relevance of race as a determinative variable in crib death, replicating the high incidence of SIDS in black children found in the much larger Naeye study, constitutes a noteworthy finding in itself.

It turned out that the deceased group varied from the controls in several ways, all of them in a direction connoting perinatal distress or biological hazard.

Table 1 presents the Apgar-score data taken from the delivery room records of the 15 SIDS cases in comparison with those of each of the control groups. It may be noted that the SIDS group's scores are lower at each of the 3 times tested than either of the controls, and that

## Table 1

Apgar Scores of SIDS Group (N=15)

Compared with Two Central Groups Matched for

Sex Alone (I) and

for Sex and Race (II)

|  | SIDS Group | Control-I | Control-II |
|---|---|---|---|
| 1 min | 6.53 | 8.47 | 8.36 |
| 2 min | 7.86 | 8.73 | 8.38 |
| 5 min | 8.67 | 9.40 | 9.00 |

First-minute Apgar Scores are significantly lower for the SIDS group than for either of the Controls. At five minutes, the SIDS group Apgar Scores are still significantly lower than Control-I.

the SIDS group at 5 minutes old has barely reached the
level of the controls as tested at one minute of age.
The differences in Apgar scores between the SIDS group
and both controls were reliable at one minute, and at
five minutes a reliable difference still existed between
the SIDS group and Control-I. The Apgar assessment
procedure is summarized in Table 2; it is a procedure for
the rapid assessment of vital function.

As shown in Table 3, there occurred interesting and
suggestive differences between the SIDS group and the two
control groups in maternal anemia during pregnancy (twice
as frequent in SIDS than in survivors), in neonatal
repiratory abnormalities noted, in the requirement of
intensive care, and in diagnosed atelectasis. Similarly,
in Table 4, it may be noted that the eventual SIDS
victims have lowered birth weights and body lengths, that
they are hospitalized significantly longer than controls,
and their serum bilirubin levels are reliably higher on
average than those of controls.

It seems clear that the infants who ultimately succumbed at 2, 3, 4, or 5 months of age were already showing, in general and on average, that they were beginning
life with some fragility. We need to know more about
that, and about the developmental processes that
transform seemingly minor insufficiencies into a morbid
crisis a few months later. I use the term "minor insufficiencies" advisedly, for the literature on crib death
in professional journals and in public documents tends to
emphasize the prior normality of SIDS victims. It
appears that while SIDS victims are essentially normal
infants, as a group they do seem to be a "risk
population" that can be identified on the basis of their
biographies. Better record-keeping and more intensive
documentation of the perinatal histories of infants
reveals a higher incidence of developmental aberration in
such infants than has often been realized.

The terms crib death and SIDS are in fact diagnoses
of essential ignorance, which is to say that the labels
are applied when no discernible sign of pathology in the
deceased infant is present. The terms are temporizing
diagnoses. They would be more useful it if were
generally appreciated that the diagnosis really means

Table 2

APGAR NEONATAL SCORING CHART

|  | 0 | 1 | 2 |
|---|---|---|---|
| Activity (muscle tone) | Flaccid | Some extremity flexion | Active motion |
| Pulse (heart rate) | None | Slow (below 100 bpm) | Over 100 bpm |
| Grimace (reflex irritability) | No response | Grimace | Strong cry |
| Appearance (color | Blue, pale | Body pink; extremities pink | Completely pink |
| Respiration (respiratory effort) | Absent | Slow | Good, crying |

After V. Apgar, 1953

Table 3

Varying Incidence of Four Perinatal Variables
for the

SIDS Group (N=15) and
Two Comparison Controls (N=15 each)

|  | SIDS Group | Control-I | Control-II |
|---|---|---|---|
| Maternal anemia during pregnancy | 12 | 6* | 6* |
| Neonatal respirator abnormality noted | 7 | 2* | 0* |
| Intensive care of newborn requied | 6 | 3 | 3 |
| Diagnosed atelectasis | 4 | 0* | 0* |

* Statistically significant in comparison with SIDS Group
by Chi-Square or Exact Probabilities Tests

## Table 4

Several Parameters Which Differentiate SIDS Cases From
Matched Controls[1]

(Standard Deviations are
Shown in Parenthses)

|  | SIDS Group | Control-I | Control-II |
|---|---|---|---|
| Birth Weight | 6.43 lbs (1.3) | 7.48 lbs** (.70) | 6.95 lbs (.94) |
| Body Length | 48.75 cm (3.18) | 51.73 cm** (1.81) | 51.08cm** (1.91) |
| Serum Bilirubin | 9.26 mg/100 ml (6.30) | 6.59* mg/100 ml (2.13) | 7.26* mg/100 ml (2.48) |
| No. days in Hospital | 11.0 (10.76) | 5.73* (1.10) | 7.27 (4.51) |

*Significant at .05 level in comparison with SIDS group
**Significant at .01 level in comparison with SIDS group

[1]Neither maternal age nor gestational age was significant.
Prematurity was  not a relevant parameter in this study.

that the cause of the death is not yet known. Research into the causes of crib death proceeds slowly.

Because of the heavy investment in pathological causation in relation to SIDS, psychophysiological theories and suppositions have not yet been sufficiently explored. Infants whose developmental histories have placed them in jeopardy, such that they require special resuscitative efforts, have lowered Apgar scores, and must remain in the hospital longer, must be assumed to have suffered some anoxic insult that is likely to subdue their activity. When infants move less, are less visually alert, feel less, suck weakly, and generally engage their environment less, they subject themselves to less opportunities for learning than "normal" infants do. In short, it is quite possible that the constellation of pathological signs found in the histories of SIDS cases is exactly such as to place them in special jeopardy from a learning deficiency.

As background for the present hypothesis, it should be recalled that death and debility resulting from inability to muster appropriate responses are not unheard of. Apart from anecdotal data readily available, such as in many instances of spouses dying shortly after the deaths of their partners, or of soldiers giving up and dying on the battlefield without apparent cause, there is the research of the leading psychobiologist, Curt Richter (1957), indicating that animals will give up in apparent despondency when confronted with life stresses that seem totally desperate. Similarly, Seligman (1975) has described the conditioning paradigms which conduce to a syndrome of helplessness and hopelessness and which can, in some conditions, lead to stupor and ultimately death. Wealthall (1976) has shown that certain types of stimulation of the nares may lead to incapacity of response and, ultimately, gross bodily debility. Shaw (1968) described very clearly the possibility of nasal obstruction as a precursor of developmental disability and crib death. In a later study, following up on a suggestion of Lipsitt which was supported in the work of Anderson and Rosenblith (1971), Swift and Emery (1973) found that inadequate response of the newborn infant to nasal occlusion is indeed related to crib death weeks later. Recently, studies of the neonatal correlates of later crib death have been hailed by Hoekelman (1976) as a significant breakthrough, especially in suggesting that crib death, when understood as a natural phenomenon, resulting from psychophysiological precursors which can be understood, will soon be much less of a mystery than has heretofore been the case. Once the deficiencies of the infant who later succumbs to crib death have been fully understood in terms of their developmental precursors and the perinatal hazards which are clearly related to these, the promise of the early studies into the causes of crib death, by Lipton and his colleagues (Lipton, 1962; Lipton, Steinschneider & Richmond, 1964), will have been realized. Recent data, including that of Naeye, Messmer, Specht, and Merritt (1976), and others, have gone so far as to suggest that even the "temperament" of the infant prior to its death may have been a contributing factor in its demise.

The period immediately following birth is one of rapid myelinization and dendritic proliferation, and this period may be an especially important one for critical learning events. Many of the unconditioned responses with which infants come into the world, such as the rooting reflex, the Babinski and Babkin responses, the grasping reflex, and others undergo marked changes between birth and about two months of age. It is not an impossible thought that humans are biologically equipped to engage in certain vital responses at birth which will diminish with the passage of time, to be supplanted by learned response systems. These learned responses become increasingly important while their ontogenetic forebears diminish in frequency and vigor.

Certain congenital response capabilities are present in the newborn which have much adaptive significance, in that they promote survival and adaptation to the biological condition of the species (Emde & Robinson, in press). The rooting reflex, for example, is a response system that is tied to feeding activity. When the infant is touched on one side of the mouth or the other, the head tends to turn ipsilaterally, whereupon mouth opening occurs and is further promoted by continuing contact with the touch stimulus. When a nipple is placed in the infant's mouth, as is usual under such circumstances, the lips close around it, a pressure seal is created, and sucking ensues in very regular rhythm dependent in part upon the shape of the intra-oral stimulus and, in addition, on the quality of the stimulation from the fluid which the infant received contingent upon its sucking behavior. The sucking response is in fact modulated in several of its dimensions by the sweetness of the fluid. The "incentives" for sucking are operative from the earliest moments after birth (Lipsitt, 1976).

It is well known that many innate response systems which are strikingly apparent at birth and soon after (e.g., the grasping reflex, the Babkin response, primitive reaching responses, and obligatory visual attention) do diminish in their frequency and intensity with the passage of time up to around two or three months of age (Paine, 1976). The firm grasp reflex, for instance, becomes a slow exploratory mode of behavior in response to the sudden pressure of an object on the palm of the hand. At least some of these response propensities are later displaced by "voluntary" learned responses mediated by higher cortical centers, perhaps in contrast to the brain-stem control that existed before experience could superimpose itself upon the lower brain function. Much brain tissue maturation occurs shortly after birth, and particularly in the first two months of human life (Dobbing, 1975; Purpura, 1975), and it may well be that this period of development is in some respects critical for the experiential accretion of certain learned responses. Could it not be that if some behavioral patterns are not adequately learned by a certain age, coinciding with the time by which the un-learned protective reflexes have diminished to an ineffective level, the organism will not have been prepared adequately for survival?

The "natural" defensive response of the normal neo-nate to respiratory occlusion, or even to the <u>threat</u> of occlusion as imposed by the presence of a covering over a part of the baby's face (as in Brazelton's scale) is for a series of defensive actions to be taken. These have been described by Lipsitt (1976), in part after a description of the pediatrician Gunther (1955, 1961) who observed such struggling of newborns while suckling at the breast. The response pattern is rather like an enraged response which escalates as the stimulus is prolonged. At birth and in the intact organism, the behavior pattern is essentially fail-safe, culminating in crying and ultimately freeing the respiratory passages (Graham, 1956).

If the newborn does not have a strong defensive response to threats to respiration, or to head restraint, it is possible that the appropriate voluntary operant behaviors will not be learned which must ultimately supplant this congenital response by around two months of age.

This supposition seems to have validity as a hypothesis, both in terms of the circumstances usually surrounding crib death and in consideration of data already available. There is good evidence, some just presented, that crib death cases have as a group begun life with some organismic deficits associated with perinatal stresses. Infants who succumb in the first year of life without any obvious fatal disease are demonstrably, as a group, mildly deficient in their responses to respiratory occlusion at birth or were in some other respect behaviorally lethargic (Anderson & Rosenblith, 1971). Moreover, the data of Steinschneider (1976) of Thoman et al. (1976), and others, point to respiratory anomalies in many histories of crib death and near-miss cases.

Crib death occurs mostly at night while others are sleeping. Such deaths are more frequent in the winter and spring months. Lower socioeconomic families are at greatest risk generally, and a cold or "sniffles" had usually been observed in the deceased infant in the few days prior to the death. Respiratory occlusion, failure of appropriate defensive behavior, and inadequate compensatory mouth-breathing when the nostrils are clogged could conceivably lead to anoxia and a comatose state, and ultimately to the infant's death, particularly when all of these conditions converge as in sleeping infants with a cold and a history of insufficient response to threatening stimulation. Such a pathway to death might involve no agonal responses whatever, as the eventual death might well have occurred in a comatose child.

It is quite possible that infants who have not learned to engage in responses necessary for clearing of the respiratory passages or clearing the way to those passages when threatened with occlusion will be those in

particular  jeopardy  at the critical ages of two to four
months.

While I am suggesting, then, that crib death may be a
developmental disability involving a learning deficit,  I
hope  that  I will not be misunderstood to be saying that
the cause of crib death is a learning disorder.   My position  is  that  in the absence of substantial data in
support of other hypotheses, and in view of  the  present
evidence  that  these  infants begin life under hazardous
conditions and have  response  aberrations,  there  is  a
reasonable  possibility of learning dysfunction.  Such an
anomaly could place disposed infants in special  jeopardy
between  two  and  four  months of  age, when there is a
marked  developmental  transition  from  involuntary
reflexive functioning in many sensory motor modalities to
responding on  a  voluntary,  deliberative,  and  learned
basis mediated by increasing cortical control.

I  wish to be clearly understood in regard to the nature  of  the  posited  learning  aberration.   No human
response  system  of which I am aware could be classified
as either solely constitutional or totally  experiential.
To  the extent that a learning anomaly is in part respon-
sible for the demise of crib-death infants, I would still
want  to  insist  upon  the  congenital or constitutional
deficit as well.  No  learning  process  can  take  place
without  the  prior  presence  of a constitutional system
that supports, and in its origin, provides the permission
for,  the  learned  response  to  occur.   Thus  it is my
position that there must have been a congenital  response
deficit present at the outset, which provided the setting
condition  for  the  deficient  respiratory  occlusion
response  to  manifest iself.   To  the extent that weak
defensive reflexes are found at birth  in  these  susceptible  infants,  the  development  of  learned  responses
necessary for the  infant  to  retrieve  its  respiratory
passages  for breathing when threatened with occlusion is
compromised.

We  must  next have studies which assess the disposi-
tion of individual infants, using criteria now  existing,
toward  undefended  hypoxic  conditions,  and see whether
providing them with a regimen  of  training  designed  to
recruit  the appropriate defensive behaviors will prevent
their demise.

## Acknowledgement

The writer is indebted to his collaborators in the study of 15 Perinatal Project crib death cases, William Q. Sturner, M.D., and Patrick M. Burke, M. D., and to Anna Christopoulos, who aided in the statistical analysis of the data. This study, and the preparation of the present manuscript, were aided substantially by a grant to the Brown University Child Study Center from the William T. Grant Foundation.

References

Anderson, R. & Rosenblith, J. F.   Sudden unexpected death syndrome:  Early indicators.  Biology of the Neonate, 1971, 18, 395-406.

Apgar, V.   A proposal for a new method of evaluation of the newborn infant.  Anesthesia and Analgesia,  1953, 32, 260.

Bergman, A. B. & Wiesner, L. A.   Relationship of passive cigarette-smoking to sudden  infant  death  syndrome. Pediatrics, 1976, 58, 665-668.

Brazelton, T. B.   Neonatal behavioral assessment scale. Philadelphia:  William Heinemann Medical Books, Ltd., 1973.

Dobbing,    J.    Human    brain    development    and    its vulnerability.   In   Mead   Johnson   Symposium   on Perinatal   and   Developmental   Medicine,   No.   6: Biological and Clinical Aspects of Brain Development, 1975, 3-12.

Emde, R. N. & Robinson, J.   The first two months:  Recent research  in  developmental  psychobiology  and  the changing  view  of  the  newborn.  In J. Noshpitz and J. Call (Eds.), Basic Handbook of Child Psychiatry,  In press.

Graham, F. K.   Behavioral differences between normal and traumatized  newborns.   I.   The   test   procedures. Psychological Monographs, 1956, 70, (20, Whole No. 427).

Gunther, M.   Instinct  and  the  nursing  couple.  The Lancet, 1955, 1, 575.

Gunther, M.   Infant behavior at the breast.  In B. Foss, (Ed.) Determinants of infant behavior.  London: Methuen and Co., 1961, 37-44.

Hoekelman, R. A.   A new perspective on sudden infant death syndrome.  American Journal of Diseases of Children, 1976, 130, 1191-1192.

Lipton, E. L. Developmental aspects of rate and rhythm in young infants. (Abstr.) Psychosomatic Medicine, 1962, 24, 517.

Lipton, E. L., Steinschneider, A., & Richmond, J. B. Autonomic function in the neonate. VIII    Cardio-pulmonary observations. Pediatrics, 1964, 3, 212-215.

Lipsitt, L. P. Developmental psychobiology comes of age: A discussion. In L. P. Lipsitt (Ed.), Developmental psychobiology:    The significance of infancy. Hillsdale, N. J.: Lawrence Erlbaum Associates, 1976, pp. 109-127.

Lipsitt, L. P., Sturner, W. Q., & Burke, P. M. Perinatal correlates of crib death. In preparation.

Naeye, R. L., Ladis, B., & Drage, J. S. Sudden infant death syndrome: A prospective study. American Journal of Diseases of Children, 1976, 130, 1207-1210.

Naeye, R. L., Messmer, J., Specht, T., & Merritt, T. A. Sudden infant death syndrome temperament before death. Behavioral Pediatrics, 1976, 88, 511-515.

Paine, R. S. The contribution of developmental neurology to child psychiatry. In E. N. Rexford, L. W. Sander, and T. Shapiro (Eds.), Infant psychiatry: A new synthesis. New Haven: Yale University Press, 1976, 26-45.

Protestos, C. D., Carpenter, R. G., McWeeny, P. M., & Emery, J. L. Obstetric and perinatal histories of children who died unexpectedly. Archives of Diseases in Childhood, 1973, 48, 835-841.

Purpura, D. P. Neuronal migration and dendritic differentiation: Normal and aberrant development of human cerebral cortex. In Mead Johnson Symposium on Perinatal and Developmental Medicine, No. 6: Biological and clinical aspects of brain development, 1975, 13-27.

Richter, C.  On the phenomenon of sudden death in animals and man.  Psychosomatic Medicine, 1957, 19, 191-198.

Seligman, M. E. P.  Helplessness.  San Francisco: W. H. Freeman, 1975.

Shaw, E. B.  Sudden unexpected death in infancy syndrome. American Journal of Diseases of Children, 1968, 2, 115-119.

Steinschneider, A.  Implications of the sudden infant death syndrome for the study of sleep in infancy. Paper presented at a symposium on crib death at meetings of the American Psychological Association, Washington, D. C., September 6, 1976.

Swift, P. G. F., & Emery, J. L.  Clinical observations of response to nasal occlusion in infancy. Archives of Diseases of Childhood, 1973, 48, 947-951.

Thoman, E., Miano, V. N., & Freese, M. P.  The role of respiratory instability in SIDS.  Paper presented in symposium on crib death at meetings of the American Psychological Association, September 6, 1976.

Wealthall, S. R.  Factors resulting in a failure to interrupt apnea.  In J. F. Bosma and J. Showacre (Eds.), Development of upper respiratory anatomy and function:  Implications for sudden infant death syndrome.  U. S. Government Printing Office, 1976, 212-225.

# Controlling Food Preferences in Children

Trygg Engen

### Self-selection Through Need?

A recent article in a publication of the National Academy of Sciences (Lifelines, September 1976) raised the question "How much lead can a child eat?" The answer is: no more than 4.5 mg lead/kg body weight per day. The fact is that many children do exceed this limit, especially those living in old and poorly maintained housing areas where the paint with high lead content put on 30 to 50 years ago is now peeling off. Eating plaster and putty contaminated with such paint can cause severe metabolic and neurological disorders. HUD, one of the world's largest landlords, has a contract out to study the possible prevention of such ingestion by addition to paint of "Bitrex" (Denatonium Benzoate), a bitter, distasteful but nontoxic substance. The assumption is that if children dislike the bitter taste of this new paint, the problem could be solved most economically by painting over the old houses to make them look good and taste bad.

The present paper will present data which are relevant in evaluating the possibility of thus reducing such a health hazard through the control of ingestion. Besides paint there are many other substances which are both harmful and generally accessible. According to reports from the National Clearing House for Poison Control (Providence Bulletin, December 16, 1976) house plants have replaced aspirin as the number one cause of poisoning in children and among poisonous plants (if eaten) are such favorites as philodendren, poinsetta, laurel, and English Ivy. The possible cause of such eating behavior, including pathological appetite for unnatural food called Pica, is usually believed to be a bodily or nutritional need. According to one recent review,

"Over a wide range of animal species there appears to be an inherent biological relationship between the taste of a substance, the acceptability or hedonic aspects of that taste, and the nutritive consequences of ingestion. In general, sweet substances are preferred by animals and are associated with positive nutritive consequences, while bitter substances are aversive and are often toxic if ingested. Salty substances are palatable or aversive and have beneficial or toxic consequences depending in part on the concentrations." (Nachman and Cole, 1971, p. 338.)

Although the emphasis in this quote is on nutrition, the significance of the taste sensation of sweet, bitter, and salty are also implied, and it is sensation that is emphasized in our research. Perhaps the pleasure of the taste sensation may lead both to eating of harmful non-foods as well as overeating of harmless foods. If bodily need were the sole determining factors of ingestion one would expect that sweets would no longer be pleasant after the body has had enough, but that obviously does not always happen. Taste is intimately related to smell in producing flavor, and it is also assumed that there are inherently pleasant and unpleasant odors.

The present problem is: Why do children eat paint and house plants? Do aspirin and philodendron taste good to a healthy child; they should not according to the quote. Perhaps it tastes good only to those suffering from some nutritional deficiency? Whatever the answer, this kind of unhealthy behavior certainly challenges the current evidence of the intellectual and sensory competence of infants (Lipsitt, 1971; Nowlis and Kessen, 1975).

The most frequently cited and classic study in this field is that by Davis (1928) on cafeteria-feeding or self-selection in children of weaning age (7-9 months). When it was left up to them, these children selected a reasonably balanced diet, presumably because their bodies knew what was needed. From a scientific point of view it is unfortunate that nothing but wholesome foods were presented in this study. It is not known what might have happened if harmful substances or even only "junk food" had been included among the available items. It should be noted that both failures as well as successes have been obtained in self-selection experiments with animals.

Clearly, Davis' results have been over-generalized. It is a curious historical fact that this cafeteria feeding experiment seemed to fit the biases or expectations of those who have written about the present topic, while an equally good paper by Gauger (1929) on the modifiability of such performance in young children has been ignored. She showed, for example, how such things as salty water and raw egg whites elicited more and more responses indicating preference with repeated exposure consistent with learning theory based on the work of Watson and others.

## Smell and Taste Preferences

While it is difficult to do self-selection test food experiments with children younger than weaning age, several experiments have been performed on simpler hedonic preference for tastes and smells. At birth, there is no firm evidence showing preference for one odor over another. In our laboratory we have found that infants averaging only two days of age detect the presence of odors such as asafoetida and anise as judged by changes in their normal regualar breathing pattern and stabilimetric activity (Engen, Lipsitt, and Kaye, 1963; see also Self, Horowitz, and Paden, 1972). Differences in the magnitude of such responses can be scored with good observer agreement. The largest response in our study was elicited by acetic acid, followed by asafoetida, phenylethyl alcohol and anise. Although one interpretation of this rank-order might be that it matches the pleasantness of the odorants, it is more likely the result of their differences in intensity. In fact, the facial and bodily reactions to all of the odors looked to us as a mild startle and escape reaction, but we have not been able to verify this.

A simliar study in Minnesota of localization showed a statistically significant tendency in two day old infants to turn away from ammonia (Rieser, Yonas, and Wikner, 1976). Ammonia, like acetic acid, is a trigeminal stimulus associated with pain and it would have been interesting to know what would have happened had a so-called pure odor such as anise been used as a control. Based on our observations, one would predict that the infants would also turn away from it.

Infants turn toward their own mother's breast pad presented on one side rather than toward that of another breastfeeding mother presented on the other side, according to a study at Oxford University (Macfarlane, 1975). This preference is apparently not innate but learned because it was not present at two days of age but becomes stronger during the first 10 days of life; at the ages of 2, 6, and 8-10 days the average percentage of times the infants turned toward mother's breast pad was 57.8, 60.3, and 68.2, respectively.

Past the neonatal period, at the age of one and two years there is some indication that odors such as dimethyl disulphide which are extremely unpleasant to adults also elicit displeasure in children (Engen and Lipsitt, unpublished data). However, even then the response is by no means firmly fixed. Except for the trigeminal stimulus of acetic acid we have yet to find an odor which seems disagreeable to all the children in any of the many groups of children we have tested. We have sampled many different odors by several different methods. In the experiment with one and two year olds the odor was blown from behind a screen with an atomizer out of view of the child. The child was seated behind the screen in front of a selection of toys. When the child was busily engaged in playing with the toys the odor or an odorless control was presented. Evidence of awareness of the odor was that it stopped the play activity and initiated characteristic facial reactions. These responses were judged by three observers who watched the child through a one-way mirror from the next room.

In addition to the dimethyl disulphide and the odorless control of water the unpleasant odor of butyric acid and the pleasant odors of amyl acetate and lavender were presented. Lavender was on the average the most preferred followed by amyl acetate, butyric acid, and dimethyl disulphide. However, this was a very weak ordering ignoring noticeable individual differences. The most striking result of this experiment was the difference between the child and the mother who was seated nearby to keep the child feeling secure. Even with the odors diluted by the greater distance from the atomizer the mother often made hedonic responses to the odors and expressed wonder why the child did not seem to care one way or the other. Compared with adults, children are quite tolerant of and oblivious to hedonic differences in odors.

Not surprisingly, as the children grow older their reactions become more similar to those of the mother and other adults. At the age of three one can derive hedonic scales from the judgment of preference for pairs of stimuli (Engen, 1974). At this age there are still great individual differences but consensus comes with age. Thus, while adults tend to agree that some odors are good and some bad, children do not. A young child may, of course, strongly dislike a particular odor but not necessarily the same one that is disliked by another child. Consequently, the possibility of using one particular foul odor to keep children away from harmful substances would be risky. An early study by Peto (1936) researched the question: "How does a child behave toward a smell which is called disgusting, or at least disagreeable by grown-up people?" Peto observed some 300 childen who were hospitalized for various reasons but well enough to participate in the experiment. He found that below the age of 5 there was essentially no evidence of displeasure with odors, and that clear evidence of displeasure appeared only after the age of 6.

While odor is supposed to dominate what is ordinarily known as flavor, taste may actually play a more inherently important role in food regulation after all. In fact, there is a striking difference in the results of taste experiments when compared to those we have described for odor. Newborn two-day old infants preferred sucrose dissolved in water over plain water as measured by the number of sucks which were recorded by a physical "sensor" in the nipple delivering the sugar and water (Engen, Lipsitt, and Peck, 1974). For matched molar concentrations sucrose was preferred over dextrose, again in representative feeding situation.

This agrees with results obtained earlier by other investigators who used the more common preference index of volume of intake (Desor, Maller and Turner, 1973; Nisbet and Gurwitz, 1970). More recently these findings have been verified again in terms of the differential tongue pressures exerted by infants when sucking various substances (Nowlis and Kessen, 1976). One has very little opportunity to learn much about tastes during the first days of life in a hospital so it is safe to assume that such preferences are innate.

However, while the results on preferences for sweets seem clear, this cannot be said for other sapid substances, particularly those assumed to be disagreeable. For the most part such research has involved bitter-tasting substances. Tentative evidence of rejection of the taste of $10^{-4}$M quinine was reported in an earlier pilot experiment by Nowlis. Steiner (1973) has presented pictures of the facial expressions indicating rejection for quinine sulphate (10.25%) as well as the sour taste of citric acid (2.5%) presented by pipette. On the other hand, Maller and Desor (1973) found the newborn infant to be indifferent to the sour, bitter, and salty tastes of urea (9.003 - 0.18M), citric acid (0.001 - 0.21M), and NaCl (0.003 - 0.20M). Although it is always possible that stronger solutions or a different method would produce different results, their experimental study, which also includes a thorough review of the experimental literature, is the most complete to date. Mallor and Desor conclude that the dislike of these substances which are unpleasant to adults, "may be contingent upon experience with these tastes, and/or maturational factors." (p. 289).

Although only anecdotal, it is interesting to note that "the wild boy of Aveyron" preferred wild fruits and natural foods which were bitter and disagreeable to the civilized French. He refused fruits, foods, and seasonings, including sugar, that seemed to them as agreeable and tasty as his selections were disagreeable and bitter (Lane, 1976, p. 323). And, if there were an innate and protective taste mechanism, one would not expect newborn babies to ingest a fatal amount of the saline solution which was, according to the news media, accidentally substituted for water in an American hospital some years ago.

As in the case of olfaction, research using older and 'domesticated' children as subjects shows clearer evidence of rejection of substances judged by adults to be disagreeable. Papousek (1967) found evidence of displeasure to a weak concentation of quinine in a head-turning experiment similar to that of Macfarlane with children ranging in age from about three to seven months.

By the age of three years children show definite taste aversions to fondant candies made too "hot" or "bitter" by adding to the normal amount of peppermint or horehound concentrations used by the candy maker (Engen and Gasparian, 1974). Since the children in the one-to-three year age bracket are the ones primarily affected by ingestion of harmful non-food substances, we had also planned an experiment involving taste in the play-situation described above for odors, but our research has come to a halt due to lack of funds. However, from the data we do have it would seem safe to assume that taste preferences would be more firmly developed than odor preferences at that age than at all the other ages we have tested bewteen two days and seven years (Engen, 1974).

## Sensory Control of Ingestion?

The remaining and crucial question is whether or not the taste of an unpleasant substance would in fact stop sucking, chewing, swallowing and, even better, initiate spitting to get rid of it. Peiper's (1963) well-known pediatric review of relevant research provides no evidence that this would happen. While there is a variety of evidence of the cognitive competence of infants, one should resist the tendency to assume that discrimination evident at birth can and will be used to control ingestion. Surely, this comes with age. Yet, among "our" children three years and older only one did not swallow candy that was disagreeable (Engen and Gasparian, 1974). Of course, this was in a social situation where a well-behaved child would not be expected to expectorate even though she had been told before-hand that to do so was part of the "game". Is it technologically possible to make a paint bitter enough so that a child would spit out a small paint chip? The real deterrent may be postingestinal as in bait-shyness (Lawless and Engen, 1976).

## Pica

It should be borne in mind that sensations represent only one of several factors controlling eating and that among these nutrition is usually considered primary. Pica presumably represents a nutritional state which produces a craving for dirt, plaster, and other unusual and sometimes harmful substances which may also contain something needed such as iron or calcium. According to Cooper (1957), pica is typically associated with lack of food or deficient diets, other illnesses and defects. Her survey of the literature and epidemiologial research calls attention to two salient conditions in the development of such strange appetites in young children. One is that bodily need is the essential factor in

determining what is craved.    Recent  research  indicates
that  such  physical needs may well modify the associated
taste  sensations  (Mower,  Mair,   and   Engen,   1977).
Cooper's  survey  of  research  with  people  and animals
supports this observation.  The other  condition  is  the
one  we  have  emphasized,  namely,  that  the  child  is
relatively free from the cultural habits and  preferences
which  determine  adult  food  selection.  Therefore, when
left to his own devices the child is more likely than  an
adult  to choose unusual substances, including non-foods,
encountered more or less at random.

Psychological  factors  may  also  play  a role.  For
example, a child left alone in a crib may become restless
and  for the lack of anything else to do may chew off the
paint on the crib.   Cooper  does  not  consider  this  a
paint  pica.  Some may mistakenly think that children eat
paint because of its sweet taste due  to  the  "sugar  of
lead"  or lead acetate. This is probably wrong because it
has been shown that rats reject this substance in any and
all  concentrations  (Mason and Safford, 1965).  Also,the
lead in paint would probably be either lead  chromate  or
lead  carbonate, both of which are almost insoluble salts
and therefore not likely to elicit taste.

## The Importance of Experience

The  study  of  pica  tends to support the hypothesis
that need determines  initial  food  selection  and  that
taste  and  odor preferences are only epiphenomena.  Like
bait-shyness, sensory likes and dislikes are consequences
of  life's eating experiences.  However, bodily need does
not  guarantee  competent  performance,  as   some   have
concluded from Davis' (1928) study.  One cannot depend on
the fact that giving children what they like will suffice
because need and preference are not merely two aspects of
one condition.  One is the result of homeostatic factors,
the other experience.  Davis' study fails to consider the
plasticity in the chemical senses so well demonstrated in
Gauger's  experiment.   Cooper's (1957) research suggests
that the risk is that the child will  become  hooked  on
dirt  or junk food because it may have a desirable though
limited  homeostatic  effect.   Dirt  may  include   some
calcium  and thus come to taste good to one who needs it.
The incidence of poor nutrition even among those who  can
afford  better  as  well  as  the apparent nutritionally
inefficient use of welfare  money  and  food  stamps  are
examples  of  how there seems to be a limit to the wisdom

of the body. Careful observation of food selection and rejection by children in the school lunch program could be quite interesting.

## Conclusion

The thinking in this field has been dominated by Davis (1928) and even more profoundly by Richter (e.g., Richter, Holt, and Barelare, 1938). This has led to the belief that bodily needs, that is, physiological factors, guarantee selection of food. It is not so. A child must learn both that bitter medicine is good and that sweets are bad. A much more balanced view is presented in the work of Young (1957), another pioneer in this field who also considers the importance of need but also the pleasures of sensations and habit, as shown in the following quote:

> "New habits tend to form in agreement with body needs, but established habits tend to persist as regulators of food selection even when the selections are out of line with bodily needs."

To leave the development of habit to the child leaves too much room for chance, the more so the younger the child. Good tastes are bred not born, and effort should be made to control what childen eat so they will prefer what is good for them rather than providing them what they want as though one is running a restaurant.

References

Cooper, M. Pica. Springfield, Illinois: Charles C. Thomas Publishers, 1957.

Davis, C. M. Self-selection of diet by newly weaned infants. American Journal of Diseases of Children, 1928, 36, 651-679.

Desor, J. A., Maller, O., & Turner, R. E. Taste in acceptance of sugars by human infants. Journal of Comparative and Physiological Psychology, 1973, 84, 496-501.

Engen, T. Methods and theory in thee study of odor preferences. In J. W. Johnston, Jr., D. G. Moulton, & A. Turk (Eds.), Human Responses to Environmental Odors, New York: Academic Press, 1974, 121-141.

Engen, T. The potential usefulness of sensations of odor and taste in keeping children away from harmful substances. Annals of the New York Academy of Sciences, 1974, 237, 224-228.

Engen, T. and Gasparian, F. E. A study of taste preferences in young children. Journal of Safety Research, 1974, 6, 114-117.

Engen, T., Lipsitt, L. P., & Kaye, H. Olfactory responses and adaptation in the human neonate. Journal of Comparative and Physiological Psychology, 1963, 56, 73-77.

Engen, T., Lipsitt, L. P., and Peck, M. B. Ability of newborn infants to discriminate sapid substances. Developmental Psychology, 1974, X, 741-744.

Gauger, M. E. The modifiability of response to taste stimuli in the preschool child. Teacher College, Columbia University. Contributions to Education, No. 348, 1929.

Lane, H. The Wild Boy of Averyron. Cambridge, Mass.: Harvard University Press, 1966.

Lawless, H. T. & Engen, T. Memory. Yearbook of Science and Technology, New York: McGraw-Hill, 1976.

Lipsitt, L. P. Infant learning. In F. A. Young and D. B. Lindsley (Eds.), Early Experience and Visual Information Processing in Perceptual and Reading Disorders. American Academy of Sciences, 1971, 382-402.

Macfarlane, A. Olfaction in the development of social preferences in the human neonate. Ciba-Foundation Symposium 33 (New Series) 1975, 103-117.

Maller, O. and Desor, J. A. Effect of taste on ingestion by human newborns. In J. F. Bosma (Ed.), Oral Sensations and Perceptions. Development in the Fetus and Infant. DHEW Publication No. (NIH) 73-546, Bethesda, Maryland, 1973, 279-291.

Mason, D. J. and Safford, H. R., III. Palatability of sugar of lead. Journal of Comparative and Physiological Psychology, 1965, 59, 94-97.

Mower, G. D., Mair, R. G., & Engen, T. Influence of internal factors on the perceived intensity and pleasantness of gustatory and olfactory stimuli. In M. Kare & O. Maller (Eds.), The Chemical Senses and Nutrition, New York: Academic Press, 1977. 103-121.

Nachman M. and Cole, L. P. Role of taste in specific hungers. In L. Beider (Ed.), Handbook of Sensory Physiology, Vol. IV/2, New York: Springer Verlag, 1971, 337-362.

Nisbet, R. and Gurwitz, S. Weight, sex, and the eating behavior of human newborns. Journal of Comparative and Physiological Psychology, 1970, 73, 245-253.

Nowlis, G. H. Taste-elicited tongue movements in newborn human infants: An approach to palatibility. In J. F. Bosma (Ed.), Oral Sensations and Perceptions. Development in the Fetus and Infant. DHEW Publication No. (NIH) 73-546, Bethesda, Maryland, 1973, 292-310.

Nowlis, G. H. & Kessen, W. Human newborns differentiate differing concentrations of sucrose and glucose. Science, 1976, 191, 865-866.

Papousek, H. Experimental studies of appetitional behavior in newborn humans and infants. In H. W. Stevenson, E. H. Hess, & H. L. Reingold (Eds.), Early Behavior: Comparative and Developmental Approaches, New York: Wiley, 1967.

Peiper, A. Cerebral Functions in Infancy and Childhood. New York: Consultants Bureau, 1963.

Peto, E. Contribution to the development of smell feeling. British Journal of Medical Psychology, 1936, 15, 314-320.

Rieser, J., Yonas, A., & Wikner, K. Radial localization of odors by human newborns. Child Development, 1976, 47, 856-859.

Richter, C. P., Holt, L. E., & Barelare, B. Nutritional requirements for normal growth and reproduction in rats studied by self-selection method. American Journal of Physiology, 1938, 122, 734-744.

Self, P. A., Horowitz, F. D., & Paden, L. Y. Olfaction in newborn infants. Developmental Psychology, 1972, 7, 349-363.

Steiner, J. E. The gustofacial response: Observations on normal and anencephalic newborn infants. In J. F. Bosma (Ed.), Oral Sensations and Perceptions. Development in the Fetus and Infant. DHEW publication No. (NIH) 73-546, Bethesda, Maryland, 1973, 254-278.

Young, P. T. Psychogenic factor regulating the feeding process. American Journal of Clinical Nutrition, 1957, 5, 154-161.

# The Critical Period Hypothesis Revisited

## Mother to Infant Social Bonding in the Neonatal Period

P. H. Leiderman

The critical period hypothesis has intrigued developmental biological scientists (Grobstein, 1969) since its introduction by embryologists around the turn of the century. Spemann (1938) and Child (1941) used the term to describe the relatively brief period early in the course of development when rapid change in organization of the embryo occurs, an interruption of which would have profound effects on the subsequent structure and function of the organism. For example, if a group of cells destined to become a limb were shifted to another locus early in the gastrulation phase of embryological development, before the critical period for limb development, they would not become a limb, but instead would develop according to the requirements of the new locus. If shifted after the critical period had been passed, the cells destined originally to become a limb would develop into a limb even though inappropriate in the new location. The critical period was the relatively brief time in which major changes in organization would occur, following which further changes are unlikely or impossible. The concept arose originally in connection with structural changes. Critical periods were thought to occur early in development and implied <u>irreversible</u> alteration.

As so frequently happens to theories in physical and biological sciences, the concept found its way into the behavioral sciences. Though this is not the place to provide a history of the adoption of the concept (Scott, 1962; Moltz, 1960; Gray, 1958), suffice to say the notion of critical period seemed firmly embedded into American behavioral science by the 1950s. Much earlier in the century, however, Freud, undoubtedly influenced by the German embryologists, strongly suggested the concept in

43

his postulation of the developmental sequence related to the sensitivity of erogenous zones (oral, anal and genital) in the young infant (Sutherland, 1963). Relationships to important individuals developed around these erogenous zones, especially the genital in the age period 4 through 7 years, giving rise to the well known oedipal complex. Maldevelopment and/or fixation on particular erogenous zones was postulated to relate to the psychopathology and/or fixed characterlogical traits later on in adulthood. Thus, these periods were "critical" in the formation of the adult personality.

The major popularizer of the concept for behavioral science was probably John Paul Scott, who in a series of papers (1962, 1974) reported his work on the social development of young pups. In Europe, however, Lorenz (1970) utilized the concept in his ethological research on the development of social bonds in precocial birds somewhat earlier (1935). In a series of experiments with the gray-legged goose he found the period 24 hours after hatching was a "critical" one for the development of following behavior for this species. Other European and American ethologists (Tinbergen, 1951; Hess, 1959, 1973) elaborated on these earlier findings, and by the 1960s the concept was fully ensconced in American behavioral science.

The critical period concept in behavioral science was initially concerned with social development. It was later extended to studies of the effects of stimulation on subsequent endocrinological and adaptive behavioral changes in rats (Denenberg, 1968; Smotherman et al., 1976; Rosenblatt, 1975). Finally, the concept was introduced as possibly relevant to human studies (Ambrose, 1963; Gray, 1958, Moltz, 1960), an application summarized in a well known paper by Caldwell in 1962. This paper opened the floodgates for the clinicians and policy makers, not to mention behavioral scientists, to apply and perhaps misapply the idea to human behavior. The criticality of early environmental experiences was sometimes so fervently stated that it seemed as if the destiny of the individual was completely determined by the time a child reached 3-4 years of age.

It should be emphasized that the critical period concept arose in connection with the development of an immature organism in relationship to environmental events, including social events. For the case of social development the construct was applied to the development of relationships of the young organism to an older adult, generally the mother of the infant (Ainsworth, 1973). More recently (Bell, 1968, 1974; Barnett et al., 1970; Brazelton, 1974) the concept also has included the development of social relationships of the adult organism to the infant. In this paper I shall not deal with the critical period as it applies to the infant's relationship to the mother, but rather shall concern myself with the construct as it is used to elucidate the development of a relationship of the mother to her infant. In particular, I shall examine the evidence as it applies to social behavior in humans, taking information from mammalian studies as necessary. Finally, I shall propose additional studies since, as one would surmise, our present knowledge is insufficient to draw firm conclusions about the critical period for the development of human maternal behavior.

In this paper, the term "critical period" should be understood to include the concepts of the sensitive and optimal periods. These terms have been used to suggest the critical period idea both nonspecifically and specifically, though with quite different implications (for details see Hess, 1959, 1973).

Optimal period suggests that a given environmental event has maximum influence at a fairly restricted point in time and/or a specific stage in the sequence of development. It implies the event has influence at other times both preceding and following the optimal period. The sensitive period implies no such sharp peak in the environmental influence but rather an extended period of time of development during which environmental events, if exceeding a threshold, will influence the organism's later behavior and/or physiology. Irreversibility implied in the use of the concept of critical period is excluded in the concept of sensitive period.

What is the evidence for a sensitive (optimal or critical) period for the social bonding or attachment between a mother and her infant? It should be obvious that the central focus of such research would likely be the "social bonding forces" accompanying the birth of an infant. Rosenblatt (1975) has been one of the most indefagitable researchers in this endeavor. Using the rat as a model system, he demonstrated that both hormonal and environmental events in the postpartum period influence the onset and maintenance of maternal behavior. He postulated a biphasic system of hormonal and behavioral components to explain the development of maternal behavior in the immediate postpartum period. The hormonal control of maternal behavior in the postpartum and immediate postpartum phase facilitated nest building, lactation and infant retrieval. He suggested that a second phase coming somewhat after parturition was under control of environmental events, including the developmental stage of the infant rat and nursing, a circumstance leading to modification of the maternal behavior quite independent of hormonal control. Thus the sensitive period for the development of maternal behavior varied for different behaviors. It appeared that four days following birth might be considered a sensitive period for the development of some of these behaviors.

The major studies for larger mammals were done by Herscher, Richmond and Moore (1963a, 1963b). They found maternal behavior in sheeps and goats was modified by separation of mother and infant in the immediate neonatal period. Periods of separation as short a time as one-half hour would modify behavior three months later. Goats and sheep who had been separated from their infants were more likely to partially reject their infants when tested after three months or be indiscriminately accepting of strange kids and lambs when compared with normal ewes and dams who are highly specific in their acceptance of their own infants. The critical period for them was three hours.

Primate studies (Suomi et al., 1972; Mason & Kenny, 1974) of sufficient rigor leave the question of sensitive periods quite unanswered. However, the evidence is clear that in at least two mammalian species there is a sensitive period for the formation of mother to infant caretaking functions and social bonds.

Let us turn now to human studies which may shed some light on whether or not there is a sensitive period postpartum for the mother to become attached or socially bonded to her infant. In a series of imaginative studies, Kennell and Klaus (Kennell et al., 1975; Klaus & Kennell, 1976, Klaus et al., 1975; Newman et al., 1976), the major proponents of the affirmative position on this point, have brought forth evidence to support the existence of just such a sensitive period. Klaus and Kennell (1976) varied the amount of contact between a mother and her neonate in the immediate postpartum period. They studied primiparous mothers with normal full-term infants, one group of whom were given their babies in bed for one hour during the first two hours after birth and for five extra hours on each of the next three days, while the other group of 14 mothers received care that is routine in most United States hospitals -- that is, there is a glimpse of the baby at birth, brief contact for identification at 6-8 hours, and then 20-30 minutes during feeding every four hours. The groups were matched for age, marital and SES statuses, and sex and weight of the infant. Random assignments were made to each group. The mother returned to the hospital some 19-32 days later for a follow-up study consisting of three types of observations: 1) standardized interviews, 2) observations of the mother's performance during a physical examination of the infant, and 3) a film study of the mother feeding her infant. Mothers in the extended contact group at one month were reported to be more reluctant to leave their infants with someone else, stood and watched carefully during the physical examination, and showed more soothing behavior when the infant cried. The analysis of the film showed more fondling and en face behavior -- that is, eye to eye contact -- for the extended contact group.

At one year the extended contact group spent a greater percentage of time assisting the physician when the infant was being examined and soothed their infants when they cried. At two years of age, five mothers were selected from each group and the linguistic behavior of the mother was evaluated. The extended contact mothers asked twice as many questions, using more words per proposition, fewer content words, more adjectives, and fewer commands than the control mothers. The implication was that such verbal behavior suggested closer social bonding of the mother to her infant.

At five years the children of the extended contact mothers had significantly higher I.Q.'s and more advanced scores in two language tests when compared to the mothers of the routine contact group.

To quote from Klaus and Kennell:

"These findings suggest that just sixteen extra hours of contact within the first three days of life affect maternal behavior for one year and possibly longer and offer support for the hypothesis of maternal sensitivity."

My conclusions would be more limited. Accepting the Klaus and Kennell data for the moment, I would conclude that under the conditions of this study (i.e. lower class, largely unmarried black mothers with specific and nonspecific social and psychological support from the institution and clinical researchers over the five-year period during involvement in the study) differential early contact may be sufficient, though not necessary, to produce changes in maternal behavior and possibly in the child's behavior. The questions of whether the early contact is necessary as well as sufficient for the observed findings and whether the effect of other factors such as marital status and SES contribute to the results were not explored in this experiment. The second point is especially important since other studies have shown socio-economic status (SES) to have special influence on maternal behavior (Tulkin, 1973a, 1973b).

Klaus and Kennell continued their studies in Guatemala. Infants in two hospitals in Guatemala City were allowed to stay with their mothers for a 45-minute period immediately after parturition. The control group was permitted the usual care which consisted of routine care very much like the practice in United States hospitals. Klaus and Kennell reported that the experimental group exhibited increased breast-feeding and weight gain and fewer infections. While the results for the two hospitals were not equivalent, these findings were interpreted to support the idea that there might be a maternal sensitive period in the immediate postpartum period.

In another study de Chateau (1976) permitted one group of mothers to have skin to skin contact during the infant's first 30 minutes of life. Maternal and infant behavior was evaluated three months later by personal interview and home observation. The early contact mothers in this study reported that they breast-fed longer, adapted more easily to the infant and had fewer problems with night feeding. These findings are perhaps indicative of greater social bonding, though more likely they are concerned with maternal caretaking behavior rather than social behavior. Early contact mothers were observed to look more steadily en face, kiss more, clean the infant less and to rock the infant less. The infants of these mothers were observed to cry less and smile more. One difference not mentioned by the authors of this study was the greater participation in the antenatal program by the extended contact mothers which could indicate these extended contact mothers were already highly committed to their infants and felt more at ease with the hospital setting.

The evidence presented by these two different research groups appears to support the notion that early contact influences subsequent maternal behavior in an urban black, unmarried mother group and in a northern, Swedish, married mother group.

Our own work on this subject began in 1966, initially in collaboration with Klaus for two years while he was at Stanford, but has continued independently since that time. We were interested in the influence of the infant on maternal behavior, particularly how absence of the infant in the neonatal period might shape subsequent maternal attitudes and behavior. However, we are also interested in the modifications of paternal behavior and so our work was somewhat more family-focused than the Kennell, Klaus and de Chateau works.

We designed our study to utilize the then extant practice of separating a premature infant from the mother until just before the infant was to be discharged from the hospital. We arranged for periodic modification of the nursery procedure in order to permit a group of mothers to participate in the caretaking of their infants. Mothers in the contact group began their touching and/or caretaking within the one to three days following the infant's birth. This group of mothers was compared to the group of mothers of prematures who experienced the typical separation, generally two to three months, and both groups were compared to a full-term sample.

Seventy-two mothers, fathers and their infants were included in this study. Basic observations consisted of interviews and questionnaires of the mothers and in some cases the father. In these interviews we were particularly interested in learning about the family relations, the commitment of the mother and father towards the infant and their feelings of competency in caretaking activities. In a measure more directly related to maternal social bonding or attachment behavior, we observed the maternal behaviors in the hospital and in the home at periodic intervals for a period of 21 months after discharge from the hospital. These observations consisted of recording selected maternal and infant behaviors at 15-second intervals for approximately 50 minutes while the mother was involved with the infant. We also measured the infant's physical and psychological growth during the same period, on the assumption that maternal behavior might be reflected in some of these performance tasks. Finally, as a longer term follow-up, we recently interviewed as many mothers as were available in the San Francisco Bay Area five to eight years after our last contact. We paid particular attention to the social relationships of the mother to her child, the mother's perception of school performance, the mother's disciplinary techniques and the infant's physical health and growth. The follow-up data to 15 months postdischarge have been reported earlier (Leiderman & Seashore, 1975) and will be reviewed briefly here. The 21-month postdischarge data, when the premature infants were approximately two years old and the full-terms were 21 months old, is reported here for the first time.

Reports in our earlier papers involved the status of mothers and infants (Leifer et al., 1972; Seashore et al., 1973; Leiderman et al., 1973) at one month and at one year. We found that early separation of mother and infant did affect maternal attitudes: there was a decrease in commitment and self-confidence of mothers in the separated group. These differences disappeared by one month postdischarge from the hospital. Maternal behavior also was modified, with less ventral-ventral contact between mother and infant in the separated group. These differences, however, disappeared by one year postdischarge. What became important in differentiating maternal behaviors at one year was SES of the family, play behavior of the infant, and gender of the infant, rather than the initial experience of separation and non-separation (see Table 1). Mothers of female infants touched and attended to their infants more than mothers of male infants. Infants who were more mobile elicited more smiles from their mothers and infants who played more engendered more attention from their mothers. High socioeconomic status mothers also paid more attention to their infants. However, given the relatively small amount of the variance accounted for, there was ample opportunity for other variables not measured in our study to account for variations in maternal behavior.

The data to be reported for 21 months post hospital discharge of the infant involves only 39 of the original 72 cases because the statistical technique of multiple regression analysis that was employed required that all the information be available on all the cases. We examined the discarded 33 cases to determine whether they differed from the remaining 39 cases in factors we had found to influence maternal behavior: type of experience (whether contact, separated, or full-term) and in age, gender, education and father's SES. Since the sample did not differ, we concluded that the 39 cases used accurately reflected the original group of 72 cases.

In the 21-month post-hospital evaluations, we found that all differences in maternal behavior among the three groups - premature separated, premature contact, and full-term - disappeared except that mothers of prematures touched and attended to their child more than mothers of full-terms, and separated mothers of prematures seemed to be especially attentive. No other maternal behaviors were differentiated either by prematurity or by the early separation experience. SES, gender and parity differences found at 11 months had also disappeared by 21 months. It would appear that subsequent postdischarge events had major influence in reducing the variations we found among groups in the first postpartum year.

Table 1

Prediction of Maternal Behaviors at 11-Month Observation
(Individual Correlations[1] with Variables
Included in Multiple Regression Analysis[2])
N=56

| Independent | Dependent Variables | | | | | |
|---|---|---|---|---|---|---|
| Variables | Maternal | | | | | |
| Initial | Behaviors | | | | | |
| Conditions | Touch | Talk | Hold | Look | Smile | Attention |
| Group (sep., con., full-term) | -.13 | +.02 | -.14 | -.08 | +.31 | +.03 |
| Birth order | -.12 | -.25 | +.18 | -.28 | +.08 | -.27 |
| Gender | +.42 (F=***) | +.03 | -.15 | +.03 | -.04 | +.24 (F=[a]) |
| Infant | | | | | | |
| Behaviors | | | | | | |
| Looking at no one | -.05 | +.22 | +.17 | +.23 | +.25 | +.22 |
| Looking at mother | +.05 | --- | -.28 | --- | -.25 | -.18 |
| Silent | +.15 | -.35 | -.05 | -.24 | +.04 | -.20 |
| Noises | --- | +.34 | +.02 | +.26 | -.05 | +.17 |
| Play | +.15 | +.21 | -.16 | +.06 | +.25 | +.35 (F=*) |
| Mobility | +.13 | +.23 | -.05 | +.16 | +.40 (F=***) | +.28 |

Table 1 (con't)

| Independent Variables | Dependent Variables | | | | | |
|---|---|---|---|---|---|---|
| | | | Maternal Behaviors | | | |
| Family | Touch | Talk | Hold | Look | Smile | Attention |
| Status | | | | | | |
| Current SES | +.16 | +.10 | -.04 | -.21 | +.31 | +.32 (F=*) |
| Mother's SES background | +.11 | +.04 | -.30 (F=$^a$) | -.11 | +.23 | +.21 |

| Variations Accounted for by All Variables | | | | | | |
|---|---|---|---|---|---|---|
| | 30% | 23% | 27% | 21% | 40% | 39% |

[1]Pearson r values: $\geq$ .22, significance of p < .05

$\geq$ .31, significance of p < .01

$\geq$ .34, significance of p < .005

[2]F values included when significant
Significance of F:     [a]p < .10

* p < .05

***p < .01

In another approach, we did a multiple regression analysis using initial conditions, maternal attitudes, maternal behaviors, and family status to predict the mental and motor performance scores on the Bayley infant test. The rationale for this approach was to ascertain whether maternal attitudes and behaviors found at an earlier time to relate to postpartum separation might have a "sleeper effect" and relate to infant performance at the end of the infant's second year. For motor performance (see Table 2) we found no independent effect of any of these variables at 21 months. For mental performance (see Table 3) we found that female infants performed better than males, and that infants of higher SES status performed better than infants of low SES status. On maternal attitude and behavior variables, infants whose mother felt closer to them (dyadization) and held them more closely did less well on infant mental tests. Early separation, prematurity, parity and birth weight did not predict mental performance score. Again it would appear that familial variables and later postpartum experiences are powerful in accounting for infant performance as well as maternal behavior.

The experience of early separation, however, did have some measurable effects, though these appear to be nonspecific, affecting the entire family rather than specific mother-infant relationships. The finding (see Table 4) of high marital discord in the 22-month period following hospital discharge was evident for the initially separated group. Gender, birth order of the infant, socioeconomic status of the family did not appear to have a major influence on parental marital discord. For the period after 22 months the families of the full-term and premature contact groups became involved in divorce, indicating the importance of events other than early maternal contact for family stability. Thus, it would appear that prematurity and early mother-infant separation had its major affect on family dynamics, especially in the first two years after discharge, with much less evidence for disruption of the mother-infant tie.

Our follow-up study at five to eight years post-hospital discharge is only suggestive because we have only mothers' reports, and have not yet examined maternal behaviors. Twenty-four families (see Table 5) were located in the San Francisco Bay Area. A semi-structured interview of the mother was conducted emphasizing her relationship to the child, the child's home and school activities, familial relationships, and current family issues (see Table 6). The interviews were coded by two assistants who did not know whether the child was from the separated, contact or full-term group.

Because of the small size of the sample it was not possible to statistically test differences between contact and separated groups. Therefore, they are presented as frequencies in Table 7. It would appear that there are no outstanding differences between these two groups on selected child and familial variables as reported by mother. Whatever the effects of early contact of mother with her infant were initially, for this sample of 14 mothers, they had virtually disappeared by the time the children reached 5-8 years of age.

The final analysis of data was to compare low SES with high SES families and premature with full-term families. Because of the confounding effect of prematurity and low SES in this subsample of 24 families (9 prematures and 3 full-terms in low SES, compared with 5 prematures and 7 full-terms in high SES group) it is not possible to completely differentiate these two effects. The only statistically significant variables are shown in Table 8. They are few in number and relate more to the child's performance than to mother's attitude or behavior. Difficulty of discipline for the premature group is the only variable perhaps indicative of maternal behavioral dysfunction.

I conclude from these data that early contact, whichbegins after the first 24 hours, does not produce major changes in maternal behavior and maternal attitudes two years post-hospital discharge in predominantly middle class suburban families. Other elements affecting the child from the time of birth, specifically SES of the family and parity and gender of the child, seem to play a much larger role in pedicting mother and infant behavior. Prematurity and early separation, however, do place the family at greater risk for maintenance of familial social bonds, leading to greater likelihood for dissolution of family ties. Thus, events prior to and following the initial birth contact of the mother with her infant in our studies play a larger role in determination of

Table 2

Prediction of Motor Performance

N=39

Regression Analysis

| Independent Variables | 1-3 Months | | 12-15 Months | | 21 Months | |
|---|---|---|---|---|---|---|
| Initial Conditions | F | r | F | r | F | r |
| Prematurity | <1 | .73 | <1 | .34 | <1 | -.34 |
| Group | - | - | <1 | .18 | <1 | .32 |
| Parity | <1 | .29 | <1 | -.06 | 1.99 | -.01 |
| Gender | <1 | .01 | 1.75 | .23 | <1 | .04 |
| Birth weight | 1.95 | .76 | <1 | .30 | <1 | .32 |
| Maternal Attitude | | | | | | |
| Commitment | <1 | .14 | 1.37 | -.04 | 2.02 | .05 |
| Dyadization | <1 | -.08 | 2.79 | -.30 | <1 | -.09 |
| Social competency | 6.49** | .41 | <1 | -.01 | <1 | .02 |

## Table 2 (con't)

| | 1-3 Months | | 12-15 Months | | 21 Months | |
|---|---|---|---|---|---|---|
| | F | r | F | r | F | r |
| **Maternal** | | | | | | |
| **Behavior** | | | | | | |
| Distal attachment | <1 | - | 3.29[a] | .35 | <1 | -.06 |
| Proximal | | | | | | |
| attachment | <1 | .26 | 1.04 | .01 | 2.60 | -.32 |
| Attention | - | - | <1 | .12 | <1 | -.13 |
| **Family** | | | | | | |
| **Status** | | | | | | |
| SES-FA | - | - | <1 | .02 | <1 | .16 |
| SES-MO | 1.68 | .06 | - | - | 1.18 | .20 |
| Total Variance | | | | | | |
| Accounted for: | .70 | | .44 | | .32 | |

[a] $= p < .10$

** $= p < .025$

Table 3

Prediction of Mental Performance

N=39

Regression Analysis

| Independent Variables | 1-3 Months | | 12-15 Months | | 21 Months | |
|---|---|---|---|---|---|---|
| Initial Conditions | F | r | F | r | F | r |
| Prematurity | $3.53^a$ | .71 | <1 | .45 | <1 | .48 |
| Group | 2.42 | .58 | <1 | .42 | 1.81 | .46 |
| Parity | <1 | .39 | <1 | .16 | <1 | .09 |
| Gender | <1 | .10 | <1 | .09 | 4.77* | .17 |
| Birth weight | <1 | .71 | 1.15 | .44 | 2.34 | .46 |
| Maternal Attitude | | | | | | |
| Commitment | <1 | .08 | $3.45^a$ | +.25 | 2.73 | .05 |
| Dyadization | <1 | -.03 | <1 | -.01 | 5.24* | -.15 |
| Social competency | 6.07** | .43 | <1 | -.01 | 1.41 | .15 |

Table 3 (con't)

| | 1-3 Months | | 12-15 Months | | 21 Months | |
|---|---|---|---|---|---|---|
| | F | r | F | r | F | r |
| **Maternal** | | | | | | |
| **Behavior** | | | | | | |
| Distal attachment | <1 | -.21 | 1.13 | .11 | <1 | -.04 |
| Proximal | | | | | | |
| attachment | <1 | .18 | <1 | -.13 | 6.96** | -.27 |
| Attention | <1 | -.06 | <1 | .31 | 2.49 | .04 |
| **Family** | | | | | | |
| **Status** | | | | | | |
| SES-FA | <1 | .30 | <1 | .33 | 6.76** | .36 |
| SES-MO | <1 | .08 | <1 | .25 | 1.18 | .24 |
| Total Variance | | | | | | |
| Accounted for: | | .71 | | .43 | | .60 |

a = p < .10

* = p < .05

** = p < .025

Table 4

Marital Discord

| Age of Child at Time of Parent's Separation | Group | Gender | Birth Order | Father SES |
|---|---|---|---|---|
| | Sep | M | Later born | Low |
| < 6 Months | Con | M | First born | Low |
| | Sep | M | Later born | Med |
| 7-12 Months | Sep | F | Later born | Low |
| | Sep | F | First born | High |
| 13-22 Months | Sep | F | First born | Med |
| | Con | F | First born | Med |

## Table 4 (con't)

| Age of Child at Time of Parent's Separation | Group | Gender | Birth Order | Father SES |
|---|---|---|---|---|
| 23-60 Months | FT | F | First born | Low |
| | FT | M | First born | High |
| > 60 Months | Con | M | Later born | Low |
| | Con | F | Later born | High |
| Total | 5 Sep | 5 M | 6 First born | 5 Low |
| | 4 Con | 6 F | 5 Later born | 3 Med |
| | 2 FT | | | 3 High |

## Table 5

### Premature Infant Follow-Up

#### Description of Sample    N=24

| | Low SES | High SES |
|---|---|---|
| Premature | N=9 | N=5 |
| Full-term | N=3 | N=7 |
| Age | 6.9 years | 6.9 years |
| | Male | Female |
| Premature | N=7 | N=7 |
| Full-term | N=7 | N=3 |
| Age | 6.7 years | 7.3 years |
| | 1st Born | Later Born |
| Premature | N=4 | N=10 |
| Full-term | N=4 | N=6 |
| Age | 6.8 years | 7.0 years |

## Table 6

| Child Variables Physical and Emotional | Child Variables Social, School | Family Variables |
|---|---|---|
| 1.  Age | Who Does Child Play with in Family? | Father's Occupation |
| 2.  Height | To Whom is Child Closest? | Affluence of House |
| 3.  Weight | How does Child Play by Self? | Is Child's Bedroom Shared? |
| 4.  Birth Order | To Whom is Child most Responsive? | Financial Problems |

## Table 6 (con't)

| Child Variables Physical and Emotional | Child Variables Social, School | Family Variables |
|---|---|---|
| 5. Child's Age at Time of Discharge | Vocabulary | Family Stresses Other than Financial |
| 6. Did Child Nap as Toddler? | Progress in School | Hours per Week Mother Works |
| 7. Sleep Pattern as Infant | Writing Level | Did Having a Premie Affect the Future of Family Planning? |
| 8. Months of Bedwetting after Toilet Training | Scholastic Performance | Age of Additional Sibling #1 |
| 9. Age Child Started Day Care | Social Performance | Age of Additional Sibling #2 |
| 10. Age Child Started Nursery School | | Marital Discord Since Birth of Child |
| 11. Activity level | | Age of Child when Parents Separated |
| 12. Attention span | | Frequency of Spankings |
| 13. | | Ease of Discipline in Comparison to Other Siblings |
| 14. | | Type of Discipline most Frequently Used |

Table 7

Follow-Up Study

| Child Variables | Premature Infants | |
| --- | --- | --- |
| | Contact (N=8) | Separated (N=6) |
| Sleep as Infant | N | N |
| Regular | 4 | 3 |
| Irregular | 4 | 3 |
| Activity Level | | |
| Quiet - average | 3 | 3 |
| Active | 3 | 3 |
| Hyperactive | 2 | 0 |
| Attention Span | | |
| Long → average | 3 | 4 |
| Short: not a problem | 2 | 2 |
| Short: problematic | 2 | 0 |
| School Progress | | |
| Normal | 4 | 3 |
| Held back | 2 | 2 |

Table 7 (con't)

| | Premature Infants | |
| --- | --- | --- |
| | Contact | Separated |
| Scholastic problem | 1 | 0 |
| Behavior problem | 1 | 0 |
| | | 1 msg. |

Familial Variables

Home Problems

| | | |
| --- | --- | --- |
| None | 5 | 3 |
| Discipline | 1 | 2 |
| "Lying" | 0 | 1 |
| Hyperactivity | 2 | 0 |

Ease of Discipline

| | | |
| --- | --- | --- |
| Easier→ equal | 4 | 4 |
| Harder | 2 | 0 |
| Very difficult | 2 | 2 |

Table 8

Follow-Up Mother-Infant Separation Study

Five - Eight Years Postpartum

Reports by Mothers

| | Differences of p < .05 | | |
|---|---|---|---|
| | Mann-Whitney U Test | | |
| Group | (N=14) | | (N=10) |
| Naps as toddler | Premie | > | Full-term |
| Needed more sleep | | | |
|     as infant | " | > | " |
| High activity | " | > | " |
| Attention | " | < | " |
| Scholastic performance | " | < | " |
| Sleep alone | " | < | " |
| More difficulty with | | | |
|     discipline | " | > | " |
| | | | |
| SES | (N=12) | | (N=12) |
| High activity | Low | > | High |
| Attention span | " | < | " |
| Writing skill | " | < | " |
| Scholastic performance | " | < | " |
| Sleep alone | " | < | " |

maternal behavior and infant development than do the events immediately following parturition.

Since, the findings in our study are somewhat at variance with other work we have reviewed a comparison might be useful. Klaus and Kennell and de Chateau were concerned with the first 24 hours of contact. The rationale for emphasizing this period lies in the clinical observations (Klaus & Kennell, 1976, p. 66) that infants born of unanesthetized mothers are in a quiet alert state in the first hours after birth, later on much they are less alert. Thus, the infant in the first hour after birth is presumably in an optimal situation to entrain the mother in a social relationship and thus solidify the social bonding between the parent and infant. In our study we were not concerned with this initial hour and therefore our studies are not strictly comparable, though the fact remains that the mothers in our study did become socially bonded whether initially separated or not.

A further difference between the Klaus and Leiderman studies is that the populations are different. With little imagination, one can visualize that the East Cleveland urban population is at one end of a continuum for nuclear family organization and the middle class Palo Alto population is at the other. (All mothers were married and living with their husbands at the time of entry into our study.) Along an economic dimension the same contrast may obtain. Thus, some of the differences in results could be due to the greater potential for gain by an economically socially deprived urban group when relatively small modifications are made in the postpartum hospital environment. In contrast, the potential for gain in the predominantly middle class population is much less, and therefore they would be less likely to benefit as much from changes in hospital lying-in practice.

A third point to be examined in comparing the studies in Sweden, Cleveland, Guatemala and Palo Alto is the emphasis by Klaus and de Chateau on breast-feeding as an index of social bonding. Breast-feeding was absent in our study. I would argue that there is no evidence that breast-feeding per se can be conceived as an index of social bonding, since it is derivative of cultural values, social and economic conditions in the family as well as individual preference. For example in traditional societies, economic and social conditions dictate breast-feeding for all young infants; variations in the social bonding process develop despite the presence of breast-feeding. Breast-feeding in Western cultures may facilitate social bonding, but it should not be construed as an index of social bonding. Since the evidence in the studies reported by Klaus and Kennell and de Chateau are most clear on the point of prolonged breast-feeding by mothers having early contact with their infants, the importance of early contact for the adequate function of a biopsychological process such as breast-feeding is obvious. No conclusion about social bonding, however, can be drawn.

For a final comparison between these two groups of studies, it should be noted that Klaus' observations were made chiefly in the hospital, while we have made home observations. It is obvious, therefore, that the studies reported cannot be directly compared. However, I would conclude that the data from the various studies suggest that although close contact in the immediate neonatal period encourages social bonding for some populations, other social and experiential factors bear such a complex relationship to maternal behavior that emphasis on the brief period of one hour of contact in the immediate postpartum period as the most important element is probably misplaced. Yet I would agree that such brief early contact might be sufficient to carry an otherwise "deprived" mother above some "threshold" for social bonding even when such an experience might have relatively little influence on mothers from less deprived backgrounds.

The question may now be raised: Is there a sensitive (critical or optimal) period for mother to infant attachment or social bonding? On clinical grounds, suggested by the studies of pregnant women by Bibring (1959, 1961) it would appear such a sensitive period occurs at the time of quickening, that is, approximately five months gestation. Given the propensity of the human organism for complex cognitions and expectations, I would believe the attachment of the mother to her infant in most instances begins much before birth and surely at the time that the mother becomes aware of the developing fetus. Birth, then, is only one incident, albeit a

significant  one,  in this relatively longstanding process
and may not have the importance for humans that  it  does
for other mammals.  For women giving birth to an unwanted
child  or  who  for  various  reasons  minimize  or  deny
pregnancy,  attachment may not occur at "quickening", but
may occur at the time of childbirth.  This  circumstance
could  obtain  for  some  of the unmarried mothers in the
Cleveland sample.  To illustrate the  complexity  of  the
problem  and  the  wide  individual  variation,  I  shall
briefly report on some unpublished data  I  collected  on
unmarried  mothers  who  were  in the process of deciding
whether or not to  see  and  hold  their  infants  before
giving  them  up  for  adoption.  Three of five elected to
see and hold their infants, while two  did  not,  fearing
they   would   become   too   attached.   This  clinical
observation   indicates   the   highly   individualistic
reactions  in  social  bonding  for women in the neonatal
period.

     Perhaps  more  directly  related  to the issue of the
effects  of childbirth on the adult human is  some  recent
work  on the effects of childbirth on father's commitment
and/or attachment to  his  young  infant.   Here  we  can
separate  contact  with  infant  from  the  birth process
itself.  We (Petersen et al., 1977) studied by  means  of
interview  and home observations fathers who participated
in the home or  hospital  birth  of  their  infants,  and
fathers  who  had  the  usual  role  of  waiting  in  the
corridors.  Fathers who  participated  in  the  birth  of
their infants at home and hospital and held their infants
immediately in the postpartum period,  appeared  to  have
greater  personal commitment to the infant as measured by
subjective report and some behavioral  observations  four
and  eight months later.  Similar observations of fathers
were made  by  Parke  (1974)  and  Greenberg  and  Morris
(1974).   While  no  case  can be made for the childbirth
process as triggering the sensitive period for attachment
for  fathers,  nonetheless,  it  is  possible  the  high
saliency of childbirth for an involved observer  such  as
father,  is sufficient to establish a social bond between
him and his child.  For discussion of neonatal attachment
as  related  to  high  saliency, a classical conditioning
model, see Hoffman and DePaulo, 1977.

     Now, in answer to the question, "Is there a sensitive
period for social bonding of human adults to an  infant?"

- the only possible response is the Scottish jurists' position when guilt or innocence cannot be determined. "Not proven" is the only verdict.

What additional evidence might be obtained which would help elucidate the experiential, temporal and situational components in the ontogenesis of social bonding for human mothers to their infants? One possibility is the study of mothers of adopted children. Since parents adopt children at different ages, one could test the hypothesis that social bonding of mother to infant varies with the age of the child. Kadushin (1967) in a study of outcome for children, reported that children adopted after age 5 seemed to make adequate adjustments to school and society. I have attempted to locate studies of adoptive parents in the American literature which contrast their parental behavior with that of natural parents and adoptive parents who later had their own natural child. I could find no such reports. If we could get data from such studies, we could test whether or not the birth process, breast-feeding, and other factors substantially modify the mother's attachment feelings and behavior towards the adopted infant or child.

In summary, there is no doubt that the critical period hypothesis has been heuristically valuable in stimulating research around important events in the development of the human organism. The ontogeny of social bonding between mother and infant is just one example. However, uncritical acceptance of as controversial a concept as the critical or sensitive period for social bonding is dangerous enough that I wish to sound a note of caution. The danger is for mothers (and fathers) who feel they have not "made it" at childbirth. They sometimes believe they cannot establish social bonds later on in the course of a relationship. Further, adoptive parents may be led to believe that they cannot become as loving or attached as natural parents because they lack a "critical experience" at an "optimal" period in the course of the infant's development. Both of these beliefs should be subject to empirical test, and for the individual case be subject to clinical evaluation. Mothers bring to the event of childbirth not only memories of their own experience with maternal care, but also culturally incorporated values and expectations.

Furthermore, maternal behaviors and attitudes are frequently symbolic of other issues. Thus, childbirth taps into many different sources, and maternal behavior is shaped by these many varied influences: it is not determined by what occurs in the perinatal period alone, but also by what is brought to the experience of childbirth, and by events beyond childbirth.

Human beings are not so inflexible and unadaptive that the initiating and fixing of a social bond must be accomplished in a very brief period following birth. On the contrary, the human organism is sufficiently complex to insure redundancy in the activation of mother-infant attachment systems. Thus, if these systems are not activated at birth, in the normal course of events, they will surely be activated within the infant's first months of life. Becoming appropriately maternal is a process emerging long before birth and continuing long thereafter. Hence what is perhaps a more important issue for researchers than elucidating whether or not there is a critical period for the initiation of social bonds is determining the necessary conditions to maintain these bonds once they have been formed. On this point, for humans at least, relatively little is known. I conclude, therefore, with the observation that there is much work to be done before we can affirm the "criticality" of any single event in the complex life of the human organism.

Acknowledgements

The initial empirical research on premature and full-term infants was supported by grants from the USPHS (HD 02636 and MH 20162/A1) and the Grant Foundation, New York.

Follow-up studies of these infants and mothers were supported by funds from Boys Town. However, the opinions expressed or the policies advocated herein do not necessarily reflect these of Boys Town.

My thanks to Dr. David Feigal for the interviewing of these mothers, to Dr. Marjorie Seashore and Ms. Rowena Hardin for statistical analyses, to Mr. Guy Reed and Ms. Due Thiemann for research assistance and to Ms. Tome Tanisawa for preparation of the manuscript.

References

Ainsworth, M. D. S. The development of infant-mother attachment. In B. M. Caldwell and H. N. Riccuti (eds.), Review of Child Development Research. Vol. 3. Chicago: University of Chicago Press, 1973.

Ambrose, J. A. The concept of a critical period for the development of social responsiveness. In B. M. Foss (ed.), Determinants of Infant Behavior 11. London: Methuen & Co., Ltd., 1963.

Barnett, C. R., Leiderman, P. H., Grobstein, R. & Klaus, M. H. Neonantal separation, the maternal side of interaction deprivation. Pediatrics, 1970, 45(2), 197-205.

Bell, R. Q. A reinterpretation of the direction of effects in studies of socialization. Psychological Review, 1968, 81-93.

Bell, R. Q. Contributions of human infants to caregiving and social interaction. In M. Lewis and L. A. Rosenblum (eds.), The Effect of the Infant on its Caregiver. New York: J. Wiley & Sons, 1974, pp. 1-20.

Bibring, G. Some considerations of the psychological processes in pregnancy. Psychoanalytic Study of the Child, 1959, 14, 113-121.

Bibring, G., Dwyer, T. F., Huntington, D. S. & Valenstein, A. F. A study of the psychological processes in pregnancy and the earliest mother-child relationship. Psychoanalytic Study of the Child, 1961, 16, 9-27.

Brazelton, T. B., Koslowski, B. & Main, M. The origins of reciprocity: The early mother-infant interaction. In M. Lewis and L. A. Rosenblum (eds.), The Effect of the Infant on its Caregiver. New York: J. Wiley & Sons, 1974, pp. 49-76.

Caldwell, B. M.   The usefulness of the critical period hypothesis in the study of filliative behavior. Merrill-Palmer Quarterly, 1962, 8, 229-242.

Child, C. M.   Patterns and Problems of Development. Chicago:  Univ. Chicago Press, 1941.

de Chateau, P.   Neonatal care routine:  Influences on maternal and infant behavior and on breast feeding. Thesis.   Umea  University Medical Dissertations, New Series #20, Umea, Sweden, 1976.

Denenberg V.   Woodcock, J. and Rosenberg, K.   Long-term effects of preweaning and postweaning.   Free environment  experience  on rats' problem-solving behavior. Journal of Comparative and Physiological Psychology, 1968, 66, 533-535.

Gray, P. H.   Theory and evidence of imprinting in human infants.   Journal of Psychology, 1958, 46, 155-166.

Greenberg, M. & Morris, N.   Engrossment:  The newborn's impact upon the father.   American   Journal   of Orthopsychiatry, 1974, 44, 520-531.

Grobstein, C.   Critical periods in development.   In N. Kretchman and D. M. Walcher (eds.), Environmental Influences on Genetic Expression, National Institute of Health:  Fogarty International.   Proc., No. 2, 1969, pp. 5-7.

Hersher, L., Richmond, J. B. & Moore, A. U.   Modifiability of critical period for the development of maternal behavior in sheep and goats.   Behavior, 1963, 20, 311-319.

Hersher, L., Richmond, J. B. & Moore, A. U.   Maternal behavior in sheep and goats.   In H. Rheingold (ed.), Maternal Behavior in Animals.   New York:  J. Wiley & Sons, 1963.

Hess, E.   The relationship between imprinting and motivation. Nebraska Symposium on Motivation.   Nebraska: University of Nebraska Press, 1959, pp. 44-77.

Hess, E.   Imprinting:  Early Experience and the Devel-
    opmental Psychobiology of Attachment.  New York:  Van
    Nostrand Reinhold, 1973, pp. 36-64, 324-350, 351-423.

Hoffman, H. S. & DePaulo, P.  Behavioral control by an
    imprinting stimulus.  American  Scientist,  1977,
    65(1), 58-66.

Kadushin, A.   Reversibility of trauma:  A follow-up of
    children adopted when older.  Social Work, 1967,
    12(4), 22-33.

Kennell, J. H., Trause, M. A. & Klaus, M. H.  Evidence
    for a sensitive period in the human mother.  In Ciba
    Foundation Symposium #33, Parent-Infant Interaction.
    Amsterdam: Elsevier, 1975.

Klaus, M. H. & Kennell, J. H.  Maternal-Infant Bonding:
    The Impact of Early Separation or Loss on Family
    Development.  St. Louis:  C. V. Mosby, Co., 1976.

Klaus, M. H., Trause, M. A. & Kennell, J. H.  Does human
    maternal behavior after delivery show a char-
    acteristic pattern?  In Ciba Foundation Symposium
    #33, Parent-Infant Interaction.  Amsterdam:
    Elsevier, 1975.

Leiderman, P. H., Leifer, A. D., Seashore, M. J.,
    Barnett, C. R. & Grobstein, R.  Mother-infant inter-
    action: Effects of early deprivation, prior
    experience and sex of infant.  In J. I. Nurnberger
    (ed.), Biological and Environmental Determinants of
    Early Development, ARNMD Vol. 51, 1973.  Baltimore:
    Williams & Wilkins, pp. 154-175.

Leiderman, P. H. & Seashore, M. J.  Mother-infant
    separation: Some delayed consequences.  In Ciba
    Foundation Symposium #33, Parent-Infant Interaction.
    Amsterdam: Elsevier, 1975.

Leifer, A. D., Leiderman, P. H., Barnett, C. R. &
    Williams, J. A.  Effects of mother-infant separation
    on maternal attachment behavior.  Child Development,
    1972, 43(4), 1203-1218.

Lorenz, K. Z. Studies in Human and Animal Behaviour. Vol. 1. Cambridge, Mass.: Harvard University Press, 1970.

Mason, W. A. & Kenney, M. D. Redirection of filial attachments in rhesus monkeys: Dogs as mother surrogates. Science, 1974, 183, 1209-1211.

Moltz, H. Imprinting: Empirical basis and theoretical significance Psychological Bulletin, 1960, 57, 291-314.

Newman, L. F., Kennell, J. H., Klaus, M. H. & Schrieber, J. M. Early Human Interactions: Mother and Child in Primary Care, Clinics in Office Practice. Philadelphia: W. B. Saunders Co., 1976, pp. 491-506.

Parke, R. Father-infant interaction. In M. H. Klaus, T. Leger and M. A. Trause (eds.), Maternal Attachment and Mothering Disorders, A Round Table Panel, Johnson & Johnson Co., Sausalito, Calif., 1974.

Peterson, G. H., Mehl, L. E. & Leiderman, P. H. The role of prenatal attitude and birth participation in determining father commitment. Unpublished manuscript, 1977.

Rosenblatt, J. S. Prepartum and postpartum regulation of maternal behavior in the rat. In Ciba Foundation Symposium Parent-Infant Interaction. Amsterdam: Elsevier, 1975.

Scott, J. P. Critical periods in behavioral development. Science, 1962, 38, 949-958.

Scott, J. P., Stewart, J. H. & DeChett, V. Critical periods in the organization of systems. Developmental Psychobiology, 1974, 7(6), 489-513.

Seashore, M. J., Leifer, A. D., Barnett, C. R. & Leiderman, P. H. The effects of denial of early mother-infant interaction on maternal self-confidence. Journal of Personality Social Psychology, 1973, 26(3), 369-378.

Smotherman, W. P., Wiener, J., Mendoza, S. P. & Levine, S. Pituitary-adrenal responsiveness of rat mothers to noxious stimuli and stimuli produced by pups. In Ciba Foundation Symposium #45, Breast-Feeding and the Mother. Amsterdam: Elsevier, 1976.

Spemann, H. Embryonic Development and Induction. New Haven: Yale University Press, 1938.

Suomi, S., Harlow, H. & McKinney, W. Monkey psychiatrists. American Journal of Psychiatry, 1972, 128 927-932.

Sutherland, J. D. The concepts of imprinting and critical period from a psychoanalytic viewpoint. In B. M. Foss (ed.), Determinants of Infant Behavior, 11, New York: J. Wiley & Sons, 1963.

Tinbergen, N. The Study of Instinct. New York: Oxford University Press, 1951.

Tulkin, S. R. Social class differences infant's reactions to mother's and stranger's voice. Developmental Psychology, 1973a, 8, 137-141.

Tulkin, S. R. Social class differences in attachment behaviors of ten-month old infants. Child Development, 1973b, 44, 171-174.

# Caretaking or Reproductive Casualty?

## Determinants in Developmental Deviancy

5

Arnold J. Sameroff

A series of reports from recent studies have found that neurological, physical, and mental characteristics of the infant during the first year of life have little relation to later behavior. Much better predictability can be obtained from social characteristics of the family. Typical results are that 25% of the variance in pre-school intelligence can be predicted with only two variables: family socio-economic status and mother's education.

The Rochester Developmental Psychopathology Study was designed to translate sociological variables into psychological variables. By the study of mother-infant interactions it should be possible to determine how social class and educational background influence the way in which mothers treat their children, and in turn how the differing ways mothers relate to their children affect their intellectual and social competencies.

Developmental outcomes are posited as being the result of complex transactions between the child and the environment in which alterations are caused by and in both components. Path analysis is a statistical technique for evaluating such complex sets of variables thought to have causal relationships.

The results of the Rochester Study using path analysis show that the largest impact on the intellectual and social competency of the pre-school child results from environmental factors transmitted through specific mother-child interaction patterns. By documenting the major role played in development by the environment, many opportunities become available for the prevention of deviancy and the fostering of competency.

This symposium is devoted to the task of identifying perinatal characteristics of human infants which will permit us to predict characteristics of those children later in life. Our society has found itself faced with a variety of clinical disturbances of children and adults which make heavy demands on the emotional resources of those in immediate contact with the disordered individuals and on the financial resources of us all. It is therefore important for us, as a society, to determine as clearly as possible the determinants of these disorders in the hope of identifying those individuals most susceptible and then, trying to prevent the occurrence of the problem.

## Continuum of reproductive casualty

It has been estimated by Babson and Benson (1971) that 300,000 children are born each year who will have learning disorders ranging from mild to severe retardation. In most cases, a lack of either a clear genetic basis or signs of clear anatomical damage in these children has been puzzling to investigators who believe in the traditional "medical model." From this point of view, if a disorder exists, there should be some clear factor in the patient's history, preferably biological, which led to his disorder. If this factor could not be found, it was presumed that the disgnostic techniques were not yet sufficiently sophisticated to detect it. Such reasoning led Gesell and Amatruda (1941) to propose the concept of minimal cerebral injury as an undetectable perinatal cause of the later learning disorder effect. Pasamanick and Knobloch (1961) expanded the range of deviant developmental outcomes thought to result from minor central nervous system dysfunctions caused by damage to the fetus or newborn child. Their results led these authors to propose a "continuum of reproductive casualty." The term casualty referred to a range of minor motor, perceptual, intellectual, learning and behavioral disabilities found in children.

Retrospective studies such as those of Pasamanick and Knobloch implicated a number of factors in early development as related to later disorder including anoxia, prematurity, and delivery complications. The major question is how these pregnancy variables play a role in producing later abnormalities.

In several publications others and I (Gottfried, 1973; Sameroff & Chandler, 1975) have extensively reviewed prospective longitudinal research which has attempted to link perinatal events and behaviors with later abnormal developmental outcomes. In these reviews we failed to find connections between perinatal events and later abnormality except in instances where there was clear evidence of neurological impairment in the newborn. We must contrast this maximal, that is, identifiable brain damage, with the elusive conceptions of minimal, that is, imperceptible brain damage which currently dominate the clinical literature. We concluded that the continuum of reproductive casualty which was thought to be positively related to the degree of abnormality present in the course of development (that is, the greater the reproductive complication, the greater the later deviancy) has not been generally supported by the data reviewed. There is a serious question as to whether a child who has suffered perinatal trauma, but showed no obvious brain damage, is at any greater risk for later deviancy than a child who has not suffered perinatal trauma.

When populations with specific perinatal complications have been studied longitudinally abnormalities have been found, but these tended to disappear with age. Postnatal anoxia may affect newborn behavior and intellectual functioning through the pre-school period, but, by school age, IQ differences between affected and control populations have all but disappeared. When infants born prematurely were followed through school age, the deficits in their intelligence at earlier ages were greatly reduced in later years.

A major conclusion of our review was that the socio-economic status of the family tended to reduce or amplify intellectual deficits. In advantaged families infants who had suffered perinatal complications generally showed no significant small residual effects at follow-up. On the other hand, many infants from lower social class homes with identical histories of complications showed significant retardations in later functioning. Social and economic status appear to have much stronger influences on the course of development than perinatal history.

An example of evidence from this last point comes from a longitudinal study of all the infants born on the island of Kauai in 1955 (Werner, Bierman, & French, 1971). The total sample of children was followed from birth; by age 10 one-third were not adequately functioning in school and had recognized physical, intellectual, or behavior problems; of this one-third who had problems at the age of 10 only a minor proportion could be attributed to the effects of serious perinatal stress. The major impact of biological defects associated with reproductive casualty appears to occur in the first weeks of pregnancy when spontaneous abortions produce many fetal losses. After this initial period, environment increasingly becomes the dominant influence. The biologically vulnerable child makes up only a small proportion of those children who will not function adequately. The authors concluded that in their study "ten times more children had problems related to the effects of poor early environment than to the effects of perinatal stress."

The conclusion of these reviews of early hazards was that in every case where a perinatal characteristic was identified as causing a later disorder, infants were found having the identical characteristic who did not develop the later disorder. Where does this leave us? There are two possibilities. The first is that we are poor experimenters and that we need to improve our methodologies if we are to find the early precursors of later disorders. The second possibility is that we are poor theoreticians and that we need to improve our approaches to understanding disorder if we are to find early precursors.

## Concepts of Person

I have opted for this second possibility and I will briefly review my reasoning. Attempts to relate earlier and later conditions in a person's life are developmental problems which require developmental approaches for analysis. Surprisingly, the solution relates to how we understand what it means to be a person. The way we answer this question will determine not only how we conceive of both abnormal and normal development, but also how we conceive of ourselves and our society. I will contrast two different answers to this question and

will try to demonstrate how these two answers lead us to
different approaches to our problem. One answer is that
a person is a mechanical object. The second answer is
that a person is a living subject. Few would admit to
defining a person as a mechanical object. Yet it is
surprising that those that would reject this view when
clearly labelled accept many less clearly labelled
concepts which place people in the mechanical object
category.

The two mechanical properties most frequently
attributed to people are (1) if an object doesn't work
right, it is because it was made wrong and, (2) objects
don't change. These two properties are related and are
found in most current views of the etiology of deviant
development. The simplest way of understanding disorder
is to say either that the disordered persons were born
that way or that some significant trauma occurred early
in their lives which so altered them, that, in effect,
they were born that way. Genetic theories of
intelligence and schizophrenia and birth complication
theories of hyperactivity are of this order. Proposing
that Blacks are not as smart as whites because they were
born with a genetically limited capacity to do abstract
thinking is another example of such thinking. People
become schizophrenic because they have a genetically
limited capacity to deal with stress. Children become
hyperactive because they suffered subtle perinatal brain
damage. Each of these theoretical relationships between
cause and effect imply that if a person has a defect,
that defect is a permanent continuing, characteristic of
that individual. In other words, both the view that human
disorders are constitutional and the view that there are
direct continuities in development between these early
defects and later deviancies are corollaries of the
belief that people are mechanical objects.

Let us turn to the second half of the phrase
"mechanical object." By the word object we imply
something which can be observed in isolation, abstracted
from its environmental context. Can we truly examine
children in such a separated state? The answer is
clearly no. From the moment of conception the genetic
material that will participate in constructing the
child's characteristics is inseparably enmeshed in a
supporting environment. The molecular biologists have

shown us that without the appropriate environmental information supplied by cytoplasmic biochemicals the genes would never get activated in the first place. Further, there is a constant transaction between the somatic and genetic material, such that a change in one is a necessary condition for subsequent changes in the other, i.e., cytoplasm turns on genes which produce chemicals which alter cytoplasm which turns on other genes in a continuing functional and structural interplay.

## Transactional Model

In a parallel development, psychologists have begun to view the development of children's mental functioning as the result of mutual transactions between the children and their experiential environment.

A distinctive feature of such a "transactional" model is the recognition given to the role children can play in modifying their environment. Our common sense understanding of how children are raised is that society takes them in hand through the agency of their parents or the school system and shapes these children to fit social expectations. But many recent studies have demonstrated that in the process of trying to shape these children the caretakers are shaped themselves. The specific characteristics of the individual child transact with the caretaker's mode of functioning to produce an individualized ongoing miniature social system.

A clear example of this situation is found in the work of Thomas, Chess, and Birch (1968) in their New York longitudinal study. These investigators were able to classify young infants into two major categories of temperament. The easy child who slept and fed regularly, was able to approach and adapt to new situations, had a high threshold to stimulation, and tended to have a positive mood was contrasted with the difficult child who had a low threshold to stimulation, high intensity responses of negative mood, irregularity of sleeping and eating, and withdrawal and poor adaptability to new situations. The mothers in the New York study had normal childrearing attitudes. However, when these normal mothers were confronted with a difficult infant, their behavior toward the child was negatively influenced.

Most of them either became anxious over their inability
to control their child's crying and irregularity or
hostile through frustration. The difficult child had
converted a formerly normal mother into an abnormal one.
The outcome of this disturbed relationship was that
nearly three times as many of the infants identified as
difficult required some professional help during
childhood as compared to other infants in the New York
study.

Of great importance in this study for the conclusions
we will come to later were the difficult infants who did
not have developmental problems. The later normalcy of
these difficult infants appeared to result from their
parents' ability to make allowances for their
temperaments. Rather than becoming anxious or hostile,
these parents regarded the infants' colicky behavior as
part of a passing stage out of which they would grow.
Thus, the fate of these difficult infants appeared to
depend on the way in which their parents responded to
them.

## Rochester Longitudinal Study

At the University of Rochester, Melvin Zax and I
(Sameroff & Zax, 1973; in press) initiated a longitudinal
study of the development from birth to four years of a
sample of about 300 infants. The mothers of the children
in our study come from diverse SES and racial
backgrounds, and included a large subsample with
emotional problems. Our two goals were first, to
identify constitutional characteristics of the infants
which would be predictive of later deviancy; and second,
to determine how the social and emotional characteristics
of the mother interacted with these constitutional
characteristics. The women in the study were seen at an
interview followed by a psychometric testing during their
pregnancy. After delivery their newborn infants were
examined in the newborn nursery with a variety of
neurological, psychophysiological, and behavioral tests.
At four and twelve months of age observers went into the
homes of these infants and using a time sampling recorded
the mother-infant interactions for periods of from four
to six hours. At four, twelve, and thirty months of age
the infants were brought into our laboratory and tested
with the Bayley Developmental Scales as well as a number

of other psychometric procedures. All of the 300 children in the study have passed through the thirty-month assessment and about 50% through four years. The data from this group will serve as a concrete example of how the transactional model described above relates to the development of the child.

We assessed the temperament of each child at four months of age. When the Mental Development Index from the Bayley Infant Scales was correlated with the temperament scores an interesting pattern appeared. The correlation between the mental test scores at four months of age and the mental test scores at thirty months of age was very small, typical of the low correlations found between these age periods in other studies (Lewis & McGurk, 1972). However, when we correlated the difficult temperament scores obtained at four months of age with the mental development scores obtained at thirty months of age, we found a highly significant correlation, i.e., the worse the temperament, the worse the mental performance. From these data we can conclude that if one wants to predict an infant's IQ score at thirty months of age from a child's behavior at four months of age, a much more reliable prediction can be made based on a report of the child's temperament than on his or her actual intellectual functioning.

What sense can we make out of this relation between difficult temperament at four months of age and poorer performance on IQ tests at thirty months of age? Is temperament a precursor of intelligence? Is it a more reliable precursor than the child's own intellectual capacities, or whatever it is we are measuring with a test at four months of age? A more rational explanation can be made using the transactional model. The child's temperament at four months of age influences how the mother is going to treat him or her in the future. The mother of a child with a difficult temperament can become turned off to that child in some way and as a consequence will not provide the stimulation and caretaking that would lead to the child's competent performance at thirty months of age. Is there any evidence to support such speculation?

In our longitudinal study intensive home observations were made of the mother-infant interactions at 12 months of age.  There were significant correlations between the child's temperament at four months of age and the mother's behavior  at home at twelve months of age. Mothers of children with difficult temperaments tended to stay away from them more, to look at them less, and to play with them less.  These same home  behaviors  of  the mother  at  12 months were negatively correlated with the child's mental development at 30 months of age.  Mothers who  stayed away from their infants and spent very little time looking at and playing with their infants at  twelve months,  tended  to have children who scored lower on the Bayley scales at thirty months of age.

One  can  see  from  these  data  that  a  low mental development score at 30 months of age  is  not  a  direct consequence  of  having  a  difficult temperament at four months  of  age  but  rather  the  result  of  a  complex transaction  with  the  environment,  in  this  case  the mother's interactive behavior.  It appears  that  infants with  difficult  temperaments  actually  do  tend to turn their mothers off in the sense that these  mothers  spend more time away from them and less time engaged with them. These are the very same maternal behaviors which seem  to be  related  to  the  child's  intellectual competence at thirty months of age.  Staying away from the infant,  not socializing,  and not engaging in play behaviors, are all related to poorer scores at the thirty-month  assessment. Although  the  ultimate  analysis  of  the  data from our longitudinal study will provide a much  richer  and  more complex  picture  of  the transactions that occur between infant and mother which produce  developmental  outcomes, these  preliminary  data  demonstrate the efficacy of the model.

In  these  examples  lies  the scientific basis for a definition of a person as a living subject:  "living" and not  mechanical  in  that there is a constant transaction between organism and environment in which both  transform each  other through their mutual interplay, and "subject" not  object  in  that  the  individual  child  cannot be isolated  from  his or her individual context, since in a different  context  the  infant  would  have  become  a different child.

These examples demonstrate the rule of constitutional variables in development.  An  innate  deficit  can  only operate at that point in development when it is manifested. Whether it will be carried on in development is determined by the environmental response. If the environment compensates for the deficiency then there is no evidence that the deficit will appear later on. On the other hand if the environment either does not compensate or acts to amplify the deficit, then one would expect to find continuing developmental problems. Where the child's vulnerability is heightened through massive or recurrent trauma only an extremely supportive environment can help to restore the normal integrative growth process. A seriously brain-damaged child requiring institutional care would be an instance of such an extreme case of reproductive casualty. On the other extreme a highly disordered caretaking setting might convert the most sturdy and integrated of children into a caretaking casualty.

## Continuity and Discontinuity

Despite the intuitive rightness of the notion that one should be able to make long-range predictions based on the initial characteristics of a child or his environment, we have found little evidence for the validity of such predictions. One view of the inadequacy of developmental predictions sees their source in the scientist's inability to locate the critical links in the causal chain leading from antecedents to consequents. This view derives from a static mechanical definition of organism-environment interaction. A mechanical definition would be that environments are necessary for the development of constitutions, but the relationship is an additive one. In the case of intelligence, for example, the supporters of this position would argue that the environment can radically affect the phenotypic range of a particular genotype but that a constant genotype places ultimate limits on that range. In the case of schizophrenics, if the environment maintains a level of stress below a certain static threshold the schizophrenia genes may never express themselves phenotypically, although the environment can never influence the threshold itself. The additive view of organism-environment interplay is similar to that found in Newtonian physics where entities may interact but do not alter each other by that interaction. Organism and environment can interact but they do not change each other's essential characteristics.

In contrast, a biological definition of organism-environment transaction is one where there is a mutual alteration in the behavior of both organism and environment. During development these alterations become organized into a hierarchy of successively more complex structures. An initial deviancy need not get transmitted into the next developmental level because there is a partial independence between levels. A general systems approach to the study of development (Bertalanffy, 1968; Pattee, 1973) may help us to understand why certain properties of lower levels do not affect the functioning of higher levels. A physiological example will clarify this point. Each organ of the body, such as the heart, is composed of parts, i.e., its tissues, which are composed of subparts, i.e., the cells. If we focus on the muscle tissue we find that many properties of the organization of the cells are very important to the structure and function of the muscle but are generally irrelevant to the function of the heart as a whole. To anthropomorphize a bit, the heart is only concerned that the muscle does its job of contracting. Whether cell A is to the right or left of cell B is a property of the muscle which is irrelevant to the primary function of the heart, which is to pump blood. Continuing up the system hierarchy, the body as a whole relates to the heart primarily in terms of its pumping property. There are many properties of the heart which are relevant to pumping but irrelevant to the rest of the body. The body as a unit is indifferent as to how the job gets done as long as it gets done.

To apply this general systems analysis to psychological functioning would require a hierarchical theory of psychological development. Such a theory has been proposed by Piaget (1960). Regretfully, many have misinterpreted Piaget's theory of stages of cognitive development as a meaning that at transition points children cease the functioning characteristic of the current stage and begin the functioning characteristic of the next stage. Such is not the case. In the biological example above without the functioning of lower levels every higher level would collapse, i.e., no cells, no heart. Similarly, in Piaget's theory of development, without the continuing function of the lower levels of cognition the higher levels could not exist. But it is also true as in the biological example that the new functional organizations at the higher levels found in later stages of development do not depend on all the properties of the lower levels.

As an example, in Piaget's theory young infants are unable to view themselves as separate from the world around them. In their primitive solipsism, they believe that if they are not seeing or hearing or touching something, that something doesn't exist. Toward the end of the second year children come to understand that objects have an existence of their own even when they are not being observed, or heard or touched. Any particular object has an infinite number of properties or relationships which differentiate it from other objects. Infants need to recognize and coordinate only a few of these properties to achieve an understanding of object permanence. For each child, any particular object may have different properties, depending on the individual child's experience with it, but each child will attain the capacity to recognize that an independent object exists. This point is made especially clear by data from infants who have physical or perceptual disabilities yet shall manage to achieve the stage of object permanence.

The next hierarchical level in Piaget's theory is the formation of mental concepts which relate a number of these permanent objects that share a common property. As before, the totality of properties the child attributes to a given object is irrelevant to reaching the stage of concept formation. All that is required is that the child recognize a single shared property. Piaget's theory of cognitive development, which is based on hierarchically organized structures, gives us a model of intelligence in which early deficits need not be transmitted from one level to another. Children who are deaf, blind, have missing limbs, or cerebral palsy all manage to progress through the stages of cognitive development.

From the systems perspective for understanding physical and mental development, we can see why a "static" additive model of organism-environment inter- action is inadequate. There may exist continuities within a given hierarchical level of the organism, i.e., cell A will always be to the left of cell B, blind infants will not see during any of their stages of cognitive development, yet these continuities within a level do not mean that the child will have deficits in the kind of functioning required at each of the succeeding levels of development.

To summarize this point, development from a biological or psychological perspective involves a continuing sequence of restructuring in which earlier structures become incorporated into new levels of organization. These new levels of organization are based on a subset of the properties of the lower levels. Deficits or abnormalities at the lower level are generally not transmitted to the higher level, since a different series of functions is relevant to the new structures.

If the above hierarchical systems definition of a person as a living subject is valid, why is it that we spend so much time searching for cause-effect continuities in development using a mechanical object model. One answer is that continuity appears obvious. Human infants at birth have all of the physical organs they will require for their functioning. What we observe as we watch development is that the child gets bigger. The proportions may change but the topography remains continuous from birth to death. It is a minor step to conclude that psychological development should follow the same continuous course. The difference is that by birth the infant's biological development has already been hierarchically organized while its psychological development is only just beginning. If human prenatal development occurred where everyone could watch instead of in the mommy's tummy, we might find it far easier to accept a segmented view of development such as seen in the growth of a butterfly from egg to larva to pupa to imago. Another answer is that it is easier. It is far easier to objectify children and search for the source of their problems in their natures than to take on the far more difficult task of exploring the total system of the child in a context of family, school, and society. Similarly, remediation is easier. If we can place the source of the problem in the child, then we can solve the problem by medicating the child rather than medicating all the parents and teachers and politicians who play such central roles in determining the child's environment.

## Continuum of Caretaking Casualty

The predictive failures found when using the "continuum of reproductive casualty" could be attributed to ignorance about missing links in the causal chains linking perinatal risk and behavioral competencies. I have argued that from a more organismic perspective, predictive inefficiency results from a lack of knowledge about the total development process. According to this view, successful predictions cannot be made on the basis of reproductive risk alone. Michael Chandler and I (Sameroff and Chandler, 1975) proposed a continuum of caretaking casualty to incorporate the environmental risk factors leading toward poor developmental outcomes. Although reproductive casualties may play an initiating role in the production of later problems, it is the caretaking environment that will determine the ultimate outcome. At one end of the caretaking continuum, supportive, compensatory and normalizing environments appear to be able to eliminate the effects of early complications. On the other end of the continuum, caretaking by deprived, stressed, or poorly educated parents tends to exacerbate early difficulties. Except for the Kauai study (Werner, et al., 1968) environmental factors have generally been ignored in research efforts aimed at finding linear chains of causality between early pregnancy and delivery complications and later deviancy.

## Socio-economic status

The data from these various longitudinal studies of prenatal and perinatal complications have yet to produce a single predictive variable more potent than the familial and socio-economic characteristics of the caretaking environment.

At the same time that perinatal influences on intellectual functioning are dissipating, environmental influences become quite prevalent. Several studies including our own have shown that significant socio-economic status differences on psychological tests appear during the third year of life (Golden, et al., 1971; Sameroff and Zax, in press).

Can socio-economic status be used as a risk predictor? If so the design of a diagnostic measure with high predictive validity would be greatly simplified. The data which provide the most powerful answer to this question come from the Collaborative Perinatal Project, a longitudinal study of about 40,000 children from birth to seven years of age (Niswander & Gordon, 1972). Broman, Nichols, and Kennedy (1975) reported on the factors effecting intelligence test scores at 4 years of age. When familial and medical perinatal variables were combined in a complex statistical analysis only mother's educational level and socio-economic index made major contributions to the resulting equation. For white males, white females, black males, and black females, the percentage of variance explained using these two variables ranged from 8 to 18%. No perinatal variable added more than 1% explained variance in any of the analyses.

The relative importance of environmental variables demonstrated by these studies is somewhat mitigated by two important factors. The first relates to the statistical value of these variables and the second to their psychological value.

Although these data from the collaborative study drive home the point that social variables are more important in the prediction of IQ than pregnancy or birth variables, the variance explained is still quite small. Even when variables from a 4-month physical assessment, an 8-month psychological assessment, and a 12-month neurological assessment were added to the analysis a maximum of only 25% of the variance in 4 year IQ was explained. The basic predictive problem is that many of the children from families of low SES do quite well cognitively while many of the children from the higher SES groups do poorly.

The psychological issue is that SES and mother's educational level are not behavioral variables. For us to understand why mothers with low SES and little education tend to have children with low IQ's, we must know something about the links between these variables.

One can make the biological argument that the connection is genetic, but that begs the question since most of the variance in children's IQ is not explained by the parental characteristics. The connection must be a psychological one based on how parents interact with their children. If we want to explain variance and thereby improve developmental prediction of intelligence, one must explore the parameters of the social interactions of caretaker and child.

A view that blames everything on environment is as one-sided as a view blaming everything on constitution. But by using environment we are able to explain a lot more than by using constitution. The reason is that the developmental process is constantly altering childrens' constitutions as they go through the stages of psychological organization. The developmental trans-formations of the environment are far slower if they occur at all. As the child achieves each new inte-gration, the same environment is there to impede or facilitate the child's experience at each new level. The maximum environmental stimulation is caricatured by the middle class mother who fills the newborn's crib with mobiles and goldfish in plastic bags, who whiles away the day playing patty-cake and peek-a-boo with the growing infant, who constantly chatters as soon as the child can vocalize words, who places the child in pre-school programs, who monitors the school system and the child's homework, and who searches out the best college for the child's final stimulating experience. In contrast, are the disorganized, lower-class families who live in an environment where there is little positive stimulation at any age. The children must not only devote themselves to psychological survival but must spend an equal share of time insuring their physical survival.

How do we get beyond the 25% of variance in developmental outcomes explained by the child's en-vironmental variables? If we adopt the biological sub-ject definition of person we would need to focus on the transactions between each child and its environment at each important stage of development. At the University of Rochester we have been making some modest beginnings at such an enterprise.

## Path Analysis of Longitudinal Data

The typical strategy used to find differences in infant behavior is to compare groups which differ on various constitutional or social dimensions. This approach has been successful in demonstrating many differences related to socio-economic status (SES). However, if one wants to understand why children behave the way they do, such a direct approach explains very little of the variability in target behaviors. For example, social class is a "sociological" variable which must be translated into "psychological" behaviors that directly affect the child. In addition to the translation of sociological variables into psychological ones, one must take account of the mutual interplay of the mothers' and infants' behaviors as they influence each other across time.

Statistical models which are adequate to interpret the complexities of developmental processes are scarce. This lack is especially felt in developmental research where there is a need to explain changes in a variety of behaviors across time. Multivariate analysis of variance provides a basis for relating a set of independent to a set of dependent variables, but does little to clarify the paths of influence between and within the two sets of variables. A more complex form of multivariate analysis is path analysis.

Path analysis is based on a series of regression analyses which attempt to tease apart the inter-relations of an array of variables. In longitudinal research a relationship between two variables at different points in time might result from a number of connections between intermediate points which would not be readily apparent. For example, infant behavior at 30 months could be influenced by the situation at 4 months through five different paths:

(1) C4 $\longrightarrow$ C30: Characteristics of the child at 30 months are the continuation of constitutional characteristics at 4 months.

(2) M4 $\longrightarrow$ C4 $\longrightarrow$ C30: 30-month characteristics are the consequence of infant characteristics at 4

months which were produced by the mother at 4 months.

(3)  M30 ———→ C30:  30-month characteristics are related only to how the mother is treating the child at 30 months.

(4)  M4 ———→M30 ——→ C30:  Mother characteristics at 4 months influence her characteristics at 30 months which then determined the child's 30 month behavior.

(5)  C4 ———→ M4 ———→ M30 ———→ C30:  This path is similarly to the last except that the mother's 4-month characteristics were influenced by the infant's characteristics at that age. This last path is an example of the transactional model of development.

Data from the on-going 30-month assessment of our Rochester sample has provided us with measures of child competency that can be used as criteria for predictions based on variables from earlier assessments of the child and mother. A set of demographic, prenatal, newborn, 4-month and 12-month variables was selected from the data provided by 100 subjects who had completed their 30-month assessment. A demonstration path analysis was performed using the 30-month Bayley Mental Developmental Index as an outcome criterion.

Within the constraints of this paper, it would be impossible to completely explicate our findings nor would such an explication be worthwhile since we have not yet reduced our set of variables to a size where all the assessment data could be included in these path analyses. However, in order to demonstrate both the power and possibilities of this approach we will deal with two aspects of the analysis.

The importance of path analysis is that two variables chosen from different points in time usually have not one, but a variety of ways in which they are related. When a subset of the variables is examined separately, for example, one can observe all the paths leading from the mother's educational level to the child's 30-month IQ. A direct influence was found at each age showing the continuing impact of the mother on her child's development. There was also a continuity in the child's behavior in which his or her IQ was serially related from 4 to 12 to 30 months of age. As a consequence the child's intelligence at each age results from a combination of prior intrinsic and extrinsic influences. As an additional factor, the mother's education was related to the child's temperament at 4-months, which produced an independent impact on the 30-month Bayley Scores; i.e., good maternal education was related to a good infant temperament which was related to a higher IQ at 30 months.

A second type of contribution that path analysis can make to data analysis is in the identification of those variables that mediate between mother and infant characteristics. In a regression analysis using a measure of the child's adaptive behavior as a criterion and only the mother's initial characteristics as pre-dictors, the mother's social incompetency, anxiety, and SES together explained (R-square) 21% of the variance in the child's behavior. When variables from the newborn, 4 and 12 month assessments were added to the predictor variables, anxiety and SES were no longer in the resulting equation. Instead they were replaced by a set of mother and infant behaviors which explained almost 50% of the variance in the criterion. The more inclusive analysis provided a more complete understanding of how children become incompetent based on the mother's actual behavior rather than her demographic description.

In the Broman et al. (1975) analysis of the Collaborative Perinatal Project described earlier, a maximum of 28% of the variance in 4-year IQ was explained using mother's education, SES, birth data, and 4, 8 and 12-month assessments of the infant. In the Rochester study over 50% of the variance in 30-month IQ was explained when additional characteristics of the mother, e.g., social competence, and of her behaviors toward the child, e.g., home observation data, were added.

These studies emphasize that developmental assess-ments cannot be based on simple notions of continuity between analogous-appearing behaviors. From the child's side, the data from the Rochester study revealed a stronger connection between 4-month infant temperament scores and 30-month Bayley MDI's than between 4 and 30-month Bayley scores (Sameroff, 1974). On the mother's side it appears that a much greater proportion of the variance can be explained using assessments of her behavior than of the child's behavior in these early years.

## Conclusion

Let us return to our initial philosophical question, "What is a person?" I suggested two possibilities when the question was raised: the first possibility was that a person is a thing, the mechanical object, the second was that a person is a human being, the living subject. How is it possible for us to confuse these two definitions of a person? How is it possible to treat what we would all consider to be human as a thing?

The above presentation has been aimed at providing an explanation for this phenomenon. When people are treated as if a constitutional anomaly remains as an unchanging individual characteristic they are being treated as a ting. When any abnormality in functioning is treated as intrinsic to that person and taken out of the social and cultural context in which that person is living, that person is being treated as a thing. The ethical considerations of such depersonalization can be left to the humanists. Of concern here are the hard data of medical and psychological research. There has yet to be demonstrated a causal connection between a constitutional variable other than clear neurological damage and any developmental outcome in personality or intelligence. This may sound like a strong statement, but it characterizes the data from myriads of longitudinal studies. Whenever retrospective research has pointed to a variable which was thought to be causal to some adverse behavioral outcome, prospective research has shown that individuals with exactly the same characteristics or experiences have not had the adverse outcome. Whether the variable be poor genes, perinatal complications, or even psychosexual trauma, individuals with these same characteristics have shown not only a lack of later deviancy but often an increased competence (Garmezy, 1974). Why is it then that in the face of this negative data we continue to believe that premature children, colicky children, or handicapped children will all have poor developmental outcomes? I would suggest it is because we do not use the appropriate developmental perspective.

The transactional model I described earlier has permitted us to obtain a realistic view of the developmental process. It is not original here, but has a rich history running through Piaget in cognition, Waddington in embryology, Hegel in philosophy, Marx in economics, and Schneirla in zoology. It is obvious to anyone who has attempted to see people as living creatures whose characteristics are the consequence of a series of mutual influences between what they began with, and what they experienced.

When change and transformation are seen to be the rules of development rather than the exceptions, then a new perspective can be given to developmental prediction. If a child is viewed as doomed because of a poor genetic, reproductive, or caretaking history we are left only with the problem of defining an optimal institutional setting for such misbegotten souls. However, if a child's characteristics are seen as the consequence of an ongoing adaptation to a particular set of life circumstances, then we are offered a multiplicity of possibilities for changing those circumstances, and thereby changing the prognosis for that child. Frequently, the effort required may exceed the energies of parents, educators, or professionals, but that does not entitle us to shift the responsibility for the condition to the child. It is only through a clear view of the developmental process that future hope for a genuine primary prevention can be derived.

## Acknowledgement

Research and preparation supported by funds from the National Institute of Mental Health and the W.J. Grant Foundation.

# References

Babson, S. G. & Benson, R. C. Management of High-risk Pregnancy and Intensive Care of the Neonate. St. Louis: Mosby, 1971.

Bertalanffy, von L. General System Theory. New York: Braziller, 1968.

Broman, S. H., Nichols, P. L., & Kennedy, W. A. Preschool IQ: Prenatal and Early Developmental Correlates. New York: Earlbaum, 1975.

Garmezy, N. The study of competence in children at risk for severe psychopathology. In E. J. Anthony & C. Koupernik (Eds.), The child in the family: Children at psychiatric risk, Vol. 3, New York: Wiley, 1974.

Gesell, A. & Armatruda, C. Developmental Diagnosis. New York: Hoeber, 1941.

Golden, M., Birns, B., Bridges, W., & Moss, A. Social class differentiation in cognitive development among black preschool children. Child Development, 1971, 42, 37-45.

Gottfried, A. W. Intellectual consequences of perinatal anoxia. Psychological Bulletin, 1973, 80, 231-242.

Lewis, M. & McGurk, H. Evaluation of infant intelligence. Science, 1972, 178, 1174-1177.

Niswander, K. R. & Gordon, M. The Collaborative Perinatal Study of the National Institute of Neurological Diseases and Stroke: The Women and their Pregnancies. Philadelphia: Saunders, 1972.

Pasamanick, B. & Knobloch, H. Epidemiologic studies on the complications of pregnancy and the birth process. In G. Caplan (Ed.), Prevention of mental disorders in children. New York: Basic Books, 1961.

Pattee, H. H. The physical basis and origin of hierarchical control. In H. H. Patte (Ed.), Hierarchy theory: The challenge of complex systems. New York: Braziller, 1973.

Piaget, J. <u>Psychology of</u> <u>Intelligence</u>. New York: Littlefield, Adams, 1960.

Sameroff, A. J. Infant risk factors in developmental deviancy. Paper presented at the meetings of the International Association for Child Psychiatry and Allied Professions, Philadelphia, July, 1974.

Sameroff, A. J. & Chandler, M. J. Reproductive risk and the continuum of caretaking casualty. In F. D. Horowitz, M. Hetherington, S. Scarr-Salapatek, & G. Siegel (Eds.), <u>Review of Child Development Research</u>, Vol. 4. Chicago: University of Chicago, 1975, pp. 187-244.

Sameroff, A. J. & Zax, M. Neonatal characteristics of offspring of schizophrenic and neurotically-depressed mothers. <u>Journal of Nervous and Mental Diseases</u>, 1973, 157, 191-199.

Sameroff, A. J. & Zax, M. In search of schizophrenia: Young offspring of schizophrenic women. In L. C. Wynne, R. Cromwell & S. Matthysse (Eds.), <u>Nature Mature of Schizophrenia: New findings and future strategies</u>. New York: Wiley, in press.

Thomas, A., Chess, S., and Birch, H. <u>Temperament and Behavior Disorders in Children</u>, New York: New York University, 1968.

Werner, E. E., Bierman, J. M., & French, F. E. <u>The Children of Kauai</u>. Honolulu: University of Hawaii, 1971.

Werner, E., Honzik, M., & Smith, R. Prediction of intelligence and achievement at ten years from twenty months pediatric and psychologic examinations. <u>Child Development</u>, 1968, 39, 1063-1075.

# 6

# Epilogue: Safeguarding the Developmental Journey

Frances Degen Horowitz

The four major papers in this volume represent a sample of current research on early development of infants and young children; they highlight the multiplicity of factors that appear to contribute to "survival" in the developmental process and in doing so offer a perspective that is at once encouraging and forbidding. It is an encouraging perspective because we are making progress in understanding; it is a forbidding perspective because we are obviously concerned here with extremely complex processes and many factors interacting with each other with the function of that interaction not presently known.

The first two papers treat rather discrete phenomena: Sudden Infant Death Syndrome and harmful ingestion; the third and fourth papers are concerned with more global phenomena - longitudinal studies of infants and their mothers or parents, trying to ferret out the factors that contribute to particular outcomes. These four papers, in their own ways, treat and extend the current major themes emerging from research on early development. The themes might be identified as follows: biological and physiological variables interact with environmental variables in affecting behavior and in determining developmental outcomes; individual differences are significant variables, which are difficult to categorize and study; productive research in the next decade is likely to require more intensive, more microscopic, and more longitudinal emphasis, than has been true of the decade that is coming to its end.

The major themes illustrated by the papers in this volume bring us to several conclusions concerning the nature of the variables and the complexities of the interactions toward which we must direct major research efforts in the next several years. It is now clear that there are no simple predictors of developmental outcome and there are no simple hazard markers that insure any particular adverse outcome. Lipsitt has suggested not only that we can begin to strip the mysteries from the tragic phenomenon of Sudden Infant Death Syndrome but that there is a convergence of evidence that implicates some respiratory component in SIDS. Respiratory difficulty seems to combine with negative factors in the pregnancy history of the mothers and in the neonatal period of the infant. Even these additions, however, do not completely account for the phenomenon. Lipsitt introduces an individual difference variable of a learning history or a learning acquisition which fails the infant at a crucial moment. By suggesting that SIDS results from a combination of physiological precursors and predispositions, combined with a learning or response performance factor Lipsitt is drawing for us the kind of complex equation of multiple factors in complex interaction that more closely approximates the complexity of the phenomenon under consideration.

Similarly, Engen has tried to make it clear that the developmental hazard of harmful ingestion is not a problem for a simple single factor analysis. Again, physiological factors combining with individual differences are implicated. Sameroff and Leiderman also focus upon a much more complex network of events to account for developmental outcome than has been characteristically described in the past.

A variety of major research efforts have contributed to the development of the point of view expressed in the current set of papers. The massive Collaborative Perinatal Project involving 44,000 pregnant women and their off-spring resulted in several reports concerning factors affecting developmental outcome of the children. Broman, Nichols, and Kennedy (1975) reviewed the data in terms of intelligence levels of the children at four years of age relative to prenatal and early developmental factors. Pregnancy protocols, labor and delivery data, neonatal measures, and subsequent behavioral and physiological examinations of the children from birth to four years were analyzed for a population of over 26,000 children to determine which variables predicted best to

I.Q. test performance at four years. While there were
many interesting specific findings of significant
correlations of individual events such as number of
prenatal visits and IQ at four, the major relationship
for intelligence test performance was found with socio-
economic class variables and parental education. But, as
Sameroff points out, socio-economic status (SES) is not
in and of itself a psychological variable. The analysis
of the behavioral components that constitute what happens
in different SES groups is one of the more important
questions challenging the current generation of
developmental investigators. Leiderman's cogent argument
that the differences between his findings and those of
other investigators concerning how crucial early contact
is for social bonding are SES factors is further support
for Sameroff's contentions.

While the challenge to dissect SES into a functional
behavioral analysis is a central one, we must be very
careful not to let the pendulum of our hypotheses swing
too far in its direction. Socio-economic status is, even
for a sociological variable, extremely gross. An
analysis of behavioral patterns that characterize
different SES groups will undoubtedly reveal some
important differences; but it will also reveal
significant similarities and overlapping distributions.
It is likely that a more discriminative definition of SES
will result in SES being a less robust variable than we
thought. This is inevitable if only from anecdotal
observations of developmental outcomes in the population.
There are some children who come out of the poorest
environments associated with low SES who "make it"; other
children grow up in ostensibly better circumstances who
are not developmental survivors. Yarrow, Rubenstein, and
Pedersen (1975) studied a group of 42 infants who were
all from lower socio-economic homes. Their observations
of mother-infant interaction and environmental
characteristics in these low SES homes revealed
significant variability from home to home but also
yielded interesting correlations showing that infants in
environments that were stimulating and contingent did
better developmentally than infants who were not in such
environments. All the environments were low SES.

We are going to make significant progress with
regard to a functional behavioral analysis of socio-

economic status in the next decade. If that advance is
to be maximally helpful it is going to have to be coupled
with progress in understanding another set of factors.
Individual differences in children have been recognized
as important variables but how they function in
interacting, or transacting with environmental variables
is not really known. There has been an encouraging rise
in interest in individual differences in the last decade
(Escalona, 1968; Horowitz, 1969; Horowitz, 1977; Murphy
and Moriarty, 1976; Thomas, et al., 1963; Thomas and
Chess, 1977; and Westman, 1973) but individual
differences like any other variable will not, by itself,
provide exceptionally powerful predictions. Rather, it
is likely that the individual differences are one part of
the equation.

One of the problems facing researchers interested in
trying to gain a better understanding of the contribution
individual differences make to the interaction of several
variables has been the availability of good measures -
and even of useful concepts. Vulnerability and coping
strategies have been suggested by Murphy and her
colleagues (Murphy and Moriarty, 1976); temperament is
another conceptual orientation offered by Thomas and
Chess (1963; 1977). The questionnaire developed by Carey
(1973) to be used by parents when their infants are
between four and eight months of age has some promising
features. The Neonatal Behavioral Assessment Scale
(Brazelton, 1973) with more refinements may prove to be a
useful measure of individual differences in the first few
days of life. Perhaps hypotheses like Lipsitt's
concerning individual learning deficiencies will stimu-
late the development of new measures of individual differences that tap into susceptibility to response
acquisition.

The most important challenge before us is to keep the
level of complexity of the phenomena seriously in mind in
designing our research. We cannot state a problem in its
most complex form and then proceed to carry out simple
minded research. This is particularly true once the
factor of individual differences is seen as an important
contributor to understanding developmental outcome. For
example, suppose one develops a measure of individual
differences and then finds that the individual
differences do not predict to a criterion variable. If

we are really serious about the interaction of individual differences and environment then we ought not to expect prediction if we only measure the indvidual differences dimension. We need, as well, to have made a measure of the relevant environmental variables and further, we need to have described how environmental variables and individual characteristics <u>interact</u>. It is the interaction as well as the known values of the variables that is crucial to really understanding developmental outcome.

In one way or another all the papers in this volume bring us to focus upon the necessity to cast a very broad net of variables on the one hand and to try to arrive at as refined measures of variables and their interactions on the other hand. If research of this kind proceeds intensively and programmatically we have reason to be optimistic about what we can come to know about our potential for safeguarding the developmental journey of more and more of our children.

## References

Brazelton, T. B. Neonatal Behavioral Assessment Scale. London: William Heinemann Medical Books, 1973.

Broman, S. H., Nichols, P. L., and Kennedy, W. A. Preschool I.Q.: Prenatal and Early Developmental Correlates. Hillsdale, N.J.: Lawrence Erlbaum Associates, 1975.

Carey, William B. Measurement of infant temperament in pediatric practice. In J. C. Westman (Ed.), Individual Differences in Children. N.Y.: Wiley, 1973, 293-306.

Escalona, S. The Roots of Individuality. Chicago, Ill.: Aldine Publishing Co., 1968.

Horowitz, F. D. Learning, developmental research, and individual differences. In L. P. Lipsitt and H. W. Reese (Eds.), Advances in Child Development and Behavior, Vol. 4. N.Y.: Academic Press, 1969, 84-126.

Horowitz, F. D. Stability and instability in the newborn infant: The quest for elusive threads. Paper delivered at meeting of the Society for Research in Child Development, New Orleans, 1977.

Murphy, L. B. and Moriarty, A. E. Vulnerability, Coping and Growth. New Haven, Conn.: Yale University Press, 1976.

Thomas, A., Birch, H. G., Chess, S., Hertzig, M. E., and Korn, S. Behavioral Individuality in Early Childhood. N.Y.: New York University Press, 1963.

Thomas, A. and Chess, S. Temperament and Development. N.Y.: Bruner/Mazel, 1977.

Westman, J. C. (Ed.), Individual Differences in Children. N.Y.: John Wiley, 1973.

Yarrow, L. J., Rubenstein, J. L., and Pedersen, F. A. Infant and Environment. N.Y.: John Wiley and Sons, 1975.

# Author Index

# Subject Index